"Anyone can say everything you've been told is a myth. The hard part is offering something better in its place. Levit has succeeded. This book is a hard-hitting, honest, and course-correcting exposé on what it really takes to be successful in business. Highly recommended."

—Michael Port, *New York Times* bestselling author of *Book Yourself Solid*

"*Blind Spots* is essential reading for a postrecessionary climate where all the rules have changed and the old ways won't work."

—Martin Yate, *New York Times* bestselling author of *Knock 'em Dead: The Ultimate Job Search Guide*

"*Blind Spots* busts success myths as it replaces them with time-tested techniques to transform yourself into a twenty-first-century winner. If you want to lift your self-image, get real in an unreal world, or bolster your resilience, this book is a resource for you!"

—Tim Sanders, *New York Times* bestselling author of *Today We Are Rich*

"*Blind Spots* shines a very bright light on the exact traits that will make you a sought after addition to any workplace."

—John Jantsch, author of *Duct Tape Marketing* and *The Referral Engine*

"Alexandra Levit tells it like it is—not how we'd like it to be—busting myth after myth along the way to get us exactly where we want to go."

—Tory Johnson, founder and CEO, Women For Hire

"Don't believe the hype! When it comes to career advancement without killing yourself, no one tells the story better than Alexandra Levit."

—Chris Guillebeau, author of *The Art of Non-Conformity*

"Alexandra Levit's myth-busting book is a straightforward, honest, and much-needed guide to succeeding in the real world of business today. Readers are sure to feel empowered by Levit's many tell-it-like-it-is anecdotes, tips, and tactics. Highly recommended."

—Lindsey Pollak, author of *Getting from College to Career: 90 Things to Do Before You Join the Real World*

"Forget all those myths of business success: they just don't work. Read Alexandra Levit's new book and learn that today, authenticity and perseverance win the race."

—Barry J. Moltz, author of *Bounce!: Failure, Resiliency, and Confidence to Achieve Your Next Great Success*

"The thought-provoking stories, staggering statistics, and candid, digestible advice Alexandra offers throughout the book reveal the secrets to career success. This is a straight-talk book that will point out what you have been buying into that is stopping you."

—Christine Hassler, author of *20 Something Manifesto*

"Alexandra Levit proves yet again that she is a thought leader of our times. Her myth-busting advice, which weaves in real-world examples, compelling research, and great storytelling, is a must read for anyone working to make it to the top in corporate America—and be happy along the way."

—Jodi Glickman, author of *Great on the Job*

BLIND SPOTS

The 10 Business Myths
You Can't Afford to Believe on
Your New Path to Success

ALEXANDRA LEVIT

BERKLEY BOOKS, NEW YORK

THE BERKLEY PUBLISHING GROUP
Published by the Penguin Group
Penguin Group (USA) Inc.
375 Hudson Street, New York, New York 10014, USA
Penguin Group (Canada), 90 Eglinton Avenue East, Suite 700, Toronto, Ontario M4P 2Y3, Canada
(a division of Pearson Penguin Canada Inc.)
Penguin Books Ltd., 80 Strand, London WC2R 0RL, England
Penguin Group Ireland, 25 St. Stephen's Green, Dublin 2, Ireland (a division of Penguin Books Ltd.)
Penguin Group (Australia), 250 Camberwell Road, Camberwell, Victoria 3124, Australia
(a division of Pearson Australia Group Pty. Ltd.)
Penguin Books India Pvt. Ltd., 11 Community Centre, Panchsheel Park, New Delhi—110 017, India
Penguin Group (NZ), 67 Apollo Drive, Rosedale, Auckland 0632, New Zealand
(a division of Pearson New Zealand Ltd.)
Penguin Books (South Africa) (Pty.) Ltd., 24 Sturdee Avenue, Rosebank, Johannesburg 2196,
South Africa

Penguin Books Ltd., Registered Offices: 80 Strand, London WC2R 0RL, England

This book is an original publication of The Berkley Publishing Group.

While the author has made every effort to provide accurate telephone numbers and Internet addresses at the time of publication, neither the publisher nor the author assumes any responsibility for errors, or for changes that occur after publication. Further, the publisher does not have any control over and does not assume any responsibility for author or third-party websites or their content.

PRINTING HISTORY
Berkley trade paperback edition / October 2011

Library of Congress Cataloging-in-Publication Data

Levit, Alexandra, 1976–
Blind spots : 10 business myths you can't afford to believe on your new path to success /
Alexandra Levit.—Berkley trade pbk. ed.
p. cm.
Includes index.
ISBN 978-0-425-24306-0
1. Career development. 2. Success in business. I. Title.
HF5381.L35627 2011
650.1—dc22
2011014162

PRINTED IN THE UNITED STATES OF AMERICA

CONTENTS

INTRODUCTION

This is not your parents' business world. It's not even your older sister's business world. The recent recession has toppled and transformed our ideas about just about everything. Massive change is afoot and many of us are still reeling from the workforce blood letting that began three years ago and the downfall of companies we thought we all respected.

If we take the time to examine the world that's rising out of the ashes, we see that a major paradigm shift is occurring. We have realized that money and manipulation will only go so far, and we've come 180 degrees from the backbiting and dirty politics that characterized the dog-eat-dog 1980s. Inside the business world, organizations and individuals are looking inward and seeking a return to traditional human values like honesty, trust, moderation, open communication, and one-on-one relationship building.

Open the newspaper or go online and you'll see what I'm talking about. Trader Joe's has become one of the most popular grocery chains in the world, but its management refuses to expand if it means giving up its homey, mom-and-pop feel. Southwest Airlines considers customer loyalty to be more important than profitability and it qualifies a customer service candidate for employment based on attitude, not experience. Stephen M. R. Covey, son of legendary business author Stephen R. Covey, just had a runaway bestseller about resurrecting trust in the business world.

Those who wish to be gainfully employed for the foreseeable future must take this transformation seriously and adapt to new ways of doing things. In this book, we're going to explore the 10 biggest myths of business success—principles that people believe to be true even though they don't work for 98 percent of all truly successful people. The time to debunk these myths is now because they are more dangerous and less viable than ever, given this postrecessionary climate of ethical scrutiny and intense competition. If adhering to these myths didn't get you places before, it really won't today, when employers want to hire people with a puritan work ethic, people who want to do their jobs well without rocking the boat too much and who are strong representatives of the organization's culture. If you want to get ahead in this values-driven environment, you can't afford to have these blind spots. You must throw away these myths, determine what will work in their place, and immediately put it to use.

With the help of this book, it won't be as hard as it sounds. I will help you hone positive traits like authenticity, perseverance, and self-awareness and I think you'll see that the suggestions I and other experts provide ring true in your own experience and make more intuitive sense than most of these myths. As legendary business author Tom Peters once told me: "Really, it's about remembering the simple things your grandmother taught you, getting through the day, and helping others get through the day." Tom was right, and so were his equally famous colleagues Dale Carnegie and Stephen R. Covey, both of whom amassed their life fortunes writing and speaking about these concepts.

You may find this book to be a bit different from others in its class. I wrote it because I was tired of reading silly theories and platitudes dispensed by business and career authors who sell their work by giving these myths credibility and by telling readers what they want to hear. Here is one thing you can count on: I will tell it like it is. I will be honest with you about what will render you successful in today's business world, not yesterday's. I refuse to give you overly provocative advice that hasn't worked for anyone I know, like quitting your job tomorrow and starting your own business the next day, or marching into your boss's office and announcing that he should appreciate your individuality.

Now that I've set the stage, let's get to it. These myths and their realities are:

Myth #1: Overnight success is possible.

Reality: Most people persevere for a long time and experience several setbacks before achieving an objective definition of success. This chapter will explore how to move your dream forward a little bit at a time and how to cope when things temporarily go south.

Myth #2: Controversy will propel your career.

Reality: Being controversial usually generates attention for a little while, but people will probably not trust you in the long term. In this chapter we'll talk about how to incorporate the tried-and-true values of honesty and authenticity into your daily work life.

Myth #3: Employers want you to be yourself.

Reality: While employers value the unique set of skills and experiences you bring to the table, they expect you to toe the line with respect to company rules and conduct. Here we'll discuss what it means to be a professional and how to be diplomatic even if someone has wronged you.

Myth #4: Being good at your job trumps everything.

Reality: You can be the most talented employee your company has ever hired, but if your contributions aren't visible and people don't value what you do, it simply won't matter. This chapter will address how to spend a little more time promoting your job and a little less time slaving over it.

Myth #5: It's best to climb the ladder as fast as possible.

Reality: Getting promoted year after year requires near-constant vigilance as well as a laser-sharp focus on work—often to the detriment of everything else in your life. Here we'll talk about why it's prudent to enjoy your time as a middle manager or individual contributor and how to make the most of this period in your life.

Myth #6: You'll get more money because you earned it.

Reality: Not everyone rakes in a six-figure salary because they played their cards right. This chapter will demonstrate how compensation is about business realities, HR mandates, and office politics—not performance—and illustrate techniques to increase yours.

Myth #7: The problem isn't you, it's the organization.

Reality: People job jump constantly because of this one, but the truth is, the same situations crop up in the business world over and over. In this chapter we'll discuss why it makes the most sense to learn self-awareness and change your own thinking and behavior instead of waiting for the company to adapt to your needs.

Myth #8: You won't get laid off; you're too essential.

Reality: Everyone is replaceable, and employees who consistently add value are let go every day. Here we'll talk about what's really behind the decision to lay people off, and you'll learn how to identify the signs and take steps to protect your job now.

Myth #9: If only you could leave corporate America, everything would be perfect.

Reality: Running a business is harder than it looks, and entrepreneurship is not for everyone. This chapter will address why many people are better off working for large companies, including the hidden perks that you don't want to live without.

Myth #10: Do what you love, and the money will follow.
Reality: Just because you have a passion for a particular area doesn't mean you will automatically make money doing it. Here we'll talk about ways to do what you love without going broke, and how and when to take smart risks and make measured progress in pursuing meaningful work.

Each chapter includes academic research, expert commentary, anecdotes from contemporary culture, and inspirational stories from people like you who either fell prey to a blind spot and had to rethink their approach, or who recognized the myth for what it was and consequently came out on top. Along the way, I'll provide specific advice for course correction that you can use immediately in your work life. I hope that by the time you finish reading, you realize that a lot of what it takes to be successful is already a part of who you are, and that you absolutely have the power to cultivate the skills and attitude that will take you wherever you want to go, now and in the future. I am looking forward to taking the journey with you.

MYTH

#1

Overnight Success
Is Possible

We are in awe of them. We are jealous of them. We love—and hate—the people who come out of nowhere to set up camp in the corner office or amass large amounts of cash and public admiration. They are the ones who catapult from obscurity to massive success in an extremely short and frantic period of time. But don't be fooled.

Overnight success is the first myth I debunk in this book because it's one of the most widely held beliefs. It's also hugely misleading, and adopting this idea that you can easily become an overnight success could actually be quite damaging for your career and life. The truth is simple. There are very few—if any—genuine cases of overnight success. The majority of successful people have dedicated themselves to a goal and persevered for a long time, experiencing several setbacks before reaching a high

7

level of achievement that is finally noticed and talked about by others.

The best modern example of the overnight success phenomenon is Susan Boyle. A Scottish singer, Susan launched her career on the world stage when she competed on *Britain's Got Talent*. Susan appeared for the first time to stares and whispers from judges and audience members who were skeptical that any woman who looked like a dowdy old maid could sing a note. However, the moment the first few bars of *Les Misérables'* "I Dreamed a Dream" were out of her mouth, perceptions started to change. By the time she finished, the audience was on its feet and the judges were singing her praises. Susan finished second place in the competition and signed with powerhouse producer Simon Cowell's Syco Music label. Her debut album, *I Dreamed a Dream*, was the fastest-selling UK debut album of all time.

Millions—possibly even billions—watched Susan Boyle's first-round performance on television and YouTube, and the international media latched on to her story of overnight success. They said that she'd never sung in public before. They said that the idea of having a singing career wasn't even on her radar and she'd entered *Britain's Got Talent* on a whim. Just a single, one-minute performance later, Susan was rubbing elbows with Meredith Vieira and her idol Donny Osmond.

Sounds fascinating, doesn't it? But this wasn't *exactly* the way it happened. As a child, Susan attended the Edinburgh Acting School and sang at churches and karaoke bars. She trained with a professional voice coach and auditioned for musicals. As recently as 1999, Susan sang "Cry Me a River" for a charity CD and spent all her savings recording a demo that she pitched to record labels. She hit the talent show circuit in a big way, taking home titles from many local competitions. *Britain's Got Talent* was the culmination of achievement in a lifetime's worth of effort to get her singing career off the ground. It didn't happen overnight. It happened over forty-eight years!

The myth of overnight success is so prevalent that we're encouraging our kids to adopt it. Following in the footsteps of fellow elementary school student Alec Greven, who wrote the bestselling book *How to Talk to Girls*, nine-year-old Alya Nuri of Fishers, Indiana, recently wrote a series of books called *Things Every Kid Should Know* about smoking, alcohol, and drugs (www.alyanuri.com). She was sure that once she became a published author and started spreading her worthwhile message, she would get rich instantly. She quickly realized, though, that "money doesn't fall from the sky" and "even if you just want to help people, you have to work hard."

While she hasn't quite reached her goal of selling thousands of books, Alya moves her dream forward a little at a time by partnering with in-kind organizations, doing media interviews, and speaking in public. Through experience and coaching from her mom, Alya is gradually learning what it takes to become the spokesperson for a cause. And Alec Greven, by the way, wasn't an overnight success either. He peddled his handwritten, three-dollar pamphlet to thousands of locals before attracting the attention of HarperCollins.

Here's the bottom line. If you haven't conquered all your life's ambitions yet, please don't get down on yourself, because chances are, the timeline you set initially was unrealistic in the context of the challenges we're all facing in business today. This chapter is about moving your dream forward a little bit at a time, through goal setting and persistence, and how to cope when things temporarily go south.

Make Gradual Progress Through Goal Setting

A pretty brunette who has lately spent her weekends trying on bridal gowns, thirty-year-old Jennifer Woofter isn't necessarily the first person you'd imagine as a powerhouse businesswoman. You might not believe that her environmental consulting firm, Strategic Sustainability Consulting (www.sustainabilityconsult ing.com), makes substantial profits with high-profile clients like American Greetings and Georgetown University. If you'd talked to Jennifer four years ago, she wouldn't have believed it either. All she knew then was that she was bored.

In the tranquil calm of the Pacific Northwest, Jennifer attended college courses surrounded by Douglas fir and red oak trees. While she appreciated the scenery at the University of Oregon, Jennifer grew restless and finished a bachelor's degree in political science in just two years. Itching for a change, Jennifer headed for the hills of southern Virginia to get a master's degree from Virginia Tech. There, she found that the two-year program she'd selected was a bit too slow for her taste, and she finished that degree early too. "It seemed a waste to spend my prime years drinking beer in a pub with my fellow grad students when I could just as easily turn around a thesis over the summer," she told me.

While in Virginia, Jennifer joined the Calvert Group, an asset management company full of people who believe that going green can be good for a company's bottom line. The firm has a unique focus on social responsibility and prides itself on being recognized by a wide range of organizations, from the U.S. Environmental Protection Agency to *Working Mother* magazine. Jennifer was happy there for a while. She was invigorated by the research and analysis aspect of her new job and loved judging companies based on their social and environmental performance.

But before long, the girl who could not sit still wanted more. "I had a little money saved, no family dependent on my income, and complete freedom," she explains. "I thought, 'Why don't I start my own business?'" The idea didn't stay theoretical as it does for so many would-be entrepreneurs. Her mind began spinning ideas about how basic social and environmental systems could be built into a business so that the owner could eventually run the initiatives on her own.

Jennifer methodically set goals for the business, one after the other, until Strategic Sustainability Consulting was a fully functioning enterprise. In her office today, Jennifer will meet with her top consultants to finish off a two-year plan that plots reasonable growth in an economic downturn, and this evening she'll sit in front of her television and sketch new marketing materials while taking in *Grey's Anatomy*. And for her wedding, Jennifer can boast of an achievement none of her friends can top: she, not her parents, is paying for the festivities.

In the process of talking about this book, Jennifer sent me her preliminary list of goals for her business, written in deceptively simple language on a wrinkled piece of notebook paper. The list included things like "write a business plan," "think of a name," and "develop a set of services." When I first saw the list, I almost laughed at how simple it was, but Jennifer was deadly serious. Within one week, she'd gone to her local Barnes & Noble, picked up a book on business plan writing, and written a first draft. She'd registered her website domain, hired a graphic designer to do her logo, and created descriptions of cool-sounding offerings like green office audits and sustainability reporting. Most people would then wait for the paperwork to be filed, but not Jennifer. She wanted to pay herself a salary within a year, so she got busy locating pro bono clients so that she could quickly build a portfolio.

Jennifer's entrepreneurial success didn't happen overnight, and it wouldn't have happened at all without her secret weapon—her goal orientation. "I'm a compulsive list-maker, and being able to check off items throughout the day helps me create a sense of momentum," she told me. "In terms of bigger projects, I know that I get discouraged when I work on something for days, so I devise little milestones along the way. When I'm able to say that I accomplished my goal of calling x number of new prospects, I really have a sense of progress." Jennifer's goals also kept her safe from the "start up and crash" phenomenon that kills so many small businesses. "Goals force me to think my ideas through," she agreed. "Once I create a work plan for a project and can accurately predict the number of steps involved, I almost never underestimate the work involved."

Have you ever noticed that successful people spend a lot of time thinking about what they want and ways they can get it? Because they understand their ideal situation and are motivated to turn their vision into reality, they are able to focus their efforts, determine how to organize their time and resources, and eliminate distractions. On the other hand, unsuccessful people tend to complain a lot about what they don't like about their lives without proactively trying to change these unpleasant aspects. The hard truth is that few of us are just handed the ingredients for a fulfilling life. In most cases, if you want them for yourself you have to go out and grab them—and your surest path is by setting goals and following through on them.

When I was doing research for this book, I heard a great story about a guy who was tasked with outshooting an archery pro. Since he was a beginner, he never came close to the pro, who could hit the bull's-eye with one arrow. The novice eventually figured out that the way to outshoot the master was simply to blindfold him and spin him around a few times so that the pro would lose sight of the target. After all, how can anyone hit a target he is unable to see? This tale explains why people who don't set goals never realize their full potential and simply drift along in life without making any real progress.

Theories abound on the best way to set goals, but research has most often supported the SMART approach of defining goals that are specific, measurable, achievable, relevant, and time-bound. The most famous study followed a group of 1950s Yale University undergraduates who were about to graduate. The researchers discovered that only 3 percent of the senior class had written goals for their future in this format. These students had also delineated the knowledge, skills, and resources essential for achieving their goals and had outlined action plans for each objective. The researchers followed the class for the next twenty years and, incredibly, found that more than 95 percent of the group's net worth was controlled by the 3 percent who had written out their goals.

I'm obviously a believer in goal setting, but this sounded crazy to me, so I dug a bit deeper and found more biological and psychological reasons that goals are so important to getting what's ultimately important to us. For one thing, goal setting appears to be hardwired in our brains. According to Dustin Wax, a productivity writer who has investigated the science of setting goals, the brain cannot distinguish between things we want and things we have. The brain treats the failure to achieve a goal the same way that it treats the loss of a valued possession, and up until the moment the goal is achieved, we have failed to achieve it. This sets up a constant tension that the brain seeks to resolve by driving us toward accomplishment.

Another reason why goals are so critical to achievement is the so-called endowment effect, which means that when we take ownership of something, we invest ourselves in it until it becomes a part of our identity. The endowment effect was illustrated in a Cornell University experiment in which researchers gave students school logo coffee mugs and then offered to trade chocolate bars for the mugs. Very few students were willing to make the trade, no matter how much they professed to like chocolate. However, when the researchers reversed the experiment, handing out chocolate and then offering to trade mugs for the candy, they found that now, few students were interested in the mugs. The key finding? *What* the students had in their possession didn't matter, it was merely the fact that they had it in the first place. In subsequent experiments, researchers found that the endowment effect doesn't require current ownership. If we have a reasonable expectation of future possession, we will start thinking of that item as a part of us. Well, this would explain why I decided what to name my new Toyota Prius before the financing had even come through. In any case, the bottom line is that establishing a goal causes us to internalize it to the degree that activities we undertake to fulfill it feel natural and necessary.

Define the Goal and Options for Achieving It

The whole world waited for what he was about to say. On a warm, breezy day in May 1961, U.S. President John F. Kennedy announced before a special joint session of Congress the very ambitious goal of landing on the moon before the end of the decade. The goal was motivated by a variety of factors, the most significant of which was to have the United States overtake the Soviet Union in the space race.

Said Kennedy to Congress as well as the planet: "I believe that this nation should commit itself to achieving the goal, before this decade is out, of landing a man on the moon and returning him safely to the earth. No single space project in this period will be more impressive to mankind, or more important for the long-range exploration of space; and none will be so difficult or expensive to accomplish."

He wasn't kidding. In 1961, only one American had even flown in space, and even the most talented NASA employees were doubtful that the United States would be setting up shop on the moon anytime soon. But Kennedy put his money where his mouth was, committing $25 billion, employing 400,000 people, and involving 20,000 industrial firms and universities.

As soon as the goal was defined and the resources were

marshaled, mission planners considered various options for accomplishing a moon landing while thinking through the risk to human life, cost, technological limitations, and astronaut skill. They talked over four possible mission modes, including direct ascent, in which a spacecraft fueled by a Nova rocket would travel directly to the moon, land, and return as a single unit. Other options were earth orbit rendezvous, in which multiple rockets would be launched independently and dock in earth orbit, and lunar orbit rendezvous (LOR), in which a spacecraft composed of modular parts would be launched. A command module would remain in orbit around the moon, while a lunar module would descend to the moon and then return to dock with the command module while still in lunar orbit. Unlike the other plans, LOR required only a small part of the spacecraft to land on the moon, thus minimizing the mass to be launched from the moon's surface for the return trip.

The decision in favor of LOR dictated the design of what became the famous Apollo spacecraft. Kennedy wasn't alive to see it, but his goal was achieved on July 20, 1969, when Apollo 11 commander Neil Armstrong stepped off the lunar module's ladder and onto the moon's surface. It was an image that will be cemented in American history forever.

In 1961, Kennedy's goal seemed downright foolish, but like all big aspirations, it wasn't quite so unfathomable once the project was properly assessed and the most reasonable option chosen. As for Kennedy, he's still remembered for his vision and courage and his role as the father of the modern space age.

Develop Your Perseverance

As I prepared to write my 2010 book, *New Job, New You: A Guide to Reinventing Yourself in a Bright New Career*, I profiled dozens of individuals who'd made major career changes. While in many ways my interviewees were very different, they did share some common traits that made their high level of achievement possible, including perseverance.

Perseverance is defined as remaining constant to a purpose, idea, or task in spite of obstacles. Some people are born with the tendency to persevere. In fact, I can already see it in my toddler son. He likes to push his wagon around our backyard, but he doesn't always have enough strength and control to move it where he wants it to go. However, instead of giving up and crying, he faithfully pushes at the wagon from different angles until it's free of the tree or fence.

Pick up any one of Horatio Alger's rags-to-riches stories and you'll be virtually hit over the head with the lesson that earlier generations didn't expect instant gratification the way we do today. If they had, we wouldn't have had the opportunity to evolve as fully as a society, with the most critical cultural and technological advances marinating over decades. We've become a society of *now, now, now*, but the truth is that most things worth having take a little bit of process and a lot of time. You shouldn't assume that if something doesn't manifest overnight it won't happen at all, and in fact, you will do wonders for your personal development if you can learn to be patient, maintain faith in your own potential, and increase your perseverance in driving important aspects of your career forward.

While it admittedly sounds a bit corny, the first step in this journey is to believe in yourself and what you want to do. If you try for a goal, but in the back of your mind you don't actually think you can accomplish it, you will wreck havoc on and sabotage your motivation. You will probably give up more easily, which will result in even poorer self-esteem. If you're like me and find that believing in yourself is sometimes challenging, you might talk to family members, friends, a psychologist, or a coach to address your doubts and insecurities head-on.

Self-awareness is a critical part of developing perseverance. Admitting that you're the type to give up on a goal before you've completed it is the first step in changing that pattern. Then, practice keeping promises to yourself by setting small goals and refusing to quit until you've achieved them.

Another component is self-control. And how do you improve that? As John Tierney reported in the *New York Times* in 2008, research from University of Miami psychologists Michael Mc-Cullough and Brian Willoughby concludes that finding your religion may be the right move, since religiosity is correlated with higher self-control. Brain scans show that when people pray, the parts of the brain responsible for self-regulation and control of attention and emotion get a major workout. If you tend toward the agnostic, you can still get the self-control benefit by meditating privately or by getting involved with an organization that shares your values.

The final component in enhancing your perseverance is to think positively. Since I hate it when people give this advice and then stop, as if it's the easiest thing in the world to do, I'm going to tell you exactly how. My first recommendation is to realize that your thoughts control your feelings and that you can choose your response to your environment. I'm going to talk more about this idea in chapter 7, but for now, suffice it to say that in recent months, I have spoken to two people who are unemployed, but while one is always lamenting the tragic turn his life is taking, the other finds something good that has happened in his job search every day. Objectively speaking, their situations are the same, but guess who is happier, and guess who will probably be more successful in the long run?

As I'll discuss in the section on surviving setbacks, because you're human and not a cartoon character, it is difficult to have a positive attitude 100 percent of the time. When something unfortunate occurs, it's natural to feel negative emotions like anger, frustration, and sadness at first. But holding on to these until they result in constant depression and anxiety will make it all that much harder to persevere at a difficult goal.

Practice, Practice, Practice!

It's common knowledge that you have to hone your craft to really succeed in it, but a little practice won't get the job done. Another reason overnight success is a myth is that it takes ten thousand hours of work to reach the top level of a particular discipline.

In his book *Outliers: The Story of Success*, one of my favorite business authors, Malcolm Gladwell, asks a compelling question: why do some people succeed, living productive lives and having an impact, while so many more never reach their potential? Gladwell is a kindred spirit when he claims that superstars don't arise out of nowhere, propelled by genius. Instead, he says: "They are invariably the beneficiaries of hidden advantages and extraordinary opportunities and cultural legacies that allow them to learn and work hard."

It was Gladwell's book that brought the work of K. Anders Ericsson to our attention. Ericsson studied classical violinists at the Berlin Academy of Music and found that it took a rehearsal regimen of several hours a day for ten years to develop their abilities. By age twenty, the top performers had accrued ten thousand hours of practice, while the good students had completed eight thousand. What's most interesting about this study is that there wasn't a single case of a violinist who had such enormous talent that she was able to cut corners on her practice time.

Have you been doing your life's work for ten thousand hours? If not, then you may be premature in thinking that great accomplishments have passed you by.

Be Sensible and Reevaluate

Imagine being on top of the highest mountain peak on earth. Your feet and hands are rubbed raw from cold, you're gulping for air, and the earth's atmosphere is so close you can taste it. For Ed Viesturs, one of the most skilled high-altitude mountaineers in the world, it's just another day at work.

Ironically, the man who has summited Annapurna, K2, and Mount Everest got his start in the flatlands of northern Illinois. I live in this area, and I'll tell you that a speed bump meets our definition of a hill. According to writer Jai Kai, Ed became interested in mountain climbing after reading the famous account of French climber Maurice Herzog. What he admired most about Herzog was his unrelenting focus on the goal at hand. Ed himself was a goal-oriented young adult himself, and before long he had devised one of the most incredible goals in the history of the sport. Ed would climb all fourteen of the world's eight-thousand-meter peaks without the aid of supplemental oxygen.

Sound nuts? Maybe, except Ed is not the type of person to be described as reckless. He's known for his sensible approach to dangerous expeditions, and when face-to-face with a mountain, he holds fast to his motto: "Getting to the top is optional, but getting down is mandatory." More than once Ed has turned around on a mountain because conditions weren't favorable and he was risking his life. In 1988, for example, he was within 180 meters of the top of Mount Everest when he returned to the safety of base camp and reevaluated his approach. Ed doesn't look at these expeditions as failures because they were undertaken as part of the journey to the end goal, which he was certain he would eventually achieve.

Though it took years longer than he thought it would, Ed never gave up on his goal. He simply retooled his approach—and kept trying—until the timing was right. In 2005, he completed the last of the fourteen climbs and celebrated with a frozen beer.

Keep the Goal in Your Back Pocket

Goals aren't always achieved in an ideal time frame, and no one knows that better than Tim Frisby. I first heard his story through writer Vic Johnson. Tim was in high school when he made the decision to play college football. But life being what it is, Tim ended up training to be a member of the 82nd Airborne in the U.S. Army instead of working out on a college campus. Tim participated in the first Gulf War and the Kosovo conflict, all the while raising a family with six children. Twenty years passed, and Tim was still sure he'd play college football someday. His family and friends thought he was way too old, but Tim just couldn't let go of his goal. He looked around for ways to make it happen.

At the age of thirty-nine, Tim retired from the army and moved his family to Columbia, South Carolina. There was nothing preventing him from enrolling as a freshman at the University of South Carolina, as midcareer folks go back for degrees all the time. What he did next, though, definitely raised some eyebrows. Tim, who was then older than most professional football players, began training with the South Carolina Gamecocks. Before long, he was competing against guys half his age for a position on a Division I college football team. Admiring his goal as well as his stamina, the coaches invited Tim back for fall drills. At the first game, against the University of Georgia, Tim "Pops" Frisby was on the field wearing Gamecock jersey #89.

People ask me from time to time: Alex, when is it time to give up on a goal that seems fruitless? Before I heard Tim's story, I might have had a different answer. Now I'm thinking that there are certain goals that successful people always keep in their back pocket while they're busy living life. If the focus is there, the opportunity to act may eventually be as well.

Haters: Take the Good, Ignore the Bad

Paul Buchheit was the twenty-third employee hired at Google and the creator and lead developer of Gmail. In a 2009 post on his blog, he discussed the evolution of Gmail: "We started working on Gmail in August or September of 2001. For a long time, almost everyone disliked it. Some people used it anyway because of the search, but they had endless complaints. Quite a few people thought that we should kill the project, or perhaps reboot it as an enterprise product with native client software. Even when we got to the point of launching it on April 1, 2004—two and a half years after starting work on it—many people inside of Google were predicting doom. The product was too weird, and nobody wants to change e-mail services. I was told that we would never get a million users."

But Paul and his team kept on trucking. The response to the new product was surprisingly positive, and gradually people outside Silicon Valley started using Gmail. At the time of Paul's post in 2009, almost a decade after the team first conceived Gmail, its competitors Yahoo! and Microsoft had more than 250 million users each worldwide for their webmail compared to close to 100 million for Gmail. But Google's younger service gained incredible ground, with its user numbers growing by more than 40 percent in a year (compared to 2 percent growth for Yahoo! and a 7 percent fall in users for Microsoft).

Paul noted valuable input from his naysayers and otherwise ignored them. He knew that Gmail was a work in progress and he set his mind to changing and improving it. And I wouldn't be surprised if he hits his million users by the time this book is published. "My expectation is that big success takes years, and there aren't many counter-examples. This notion of overnight success is very misleading. If you're starting something new, expect a long journey. That's no excuse to move slowly though. To the contrary, you must move very fast. Otherwise you will never arrive."

Expect Some Defeat

Abraham Lincoln is widely considered to be the most admired president in the history of the United States of America. Listening to the Gettysburg Address or talking to your high school teachers, you'd think he could do no wrong. Except he could, and he did. Let's take a look at Honest Abe's lifetime record:

- Failed in business (age 22)

- Defeated in legislative run (age 23)

- Failed in business, again (age 24)

- Sweetheart died (age 26)

- Had a nervous breakdown (age 27)

- Defeated for Speaker of the House (age 29)

- Defeated for Elector (age 31)

- Defeated for Congress (age 34)

- Defeated for Congress (age 39)

- Defeated for Senate (age 46)

- Defeated for Vice President (age 47)

- Defeated for Senate (age 49)

Lincoln was elected president at the age of fifty-one, by which time he had suffered twelve major defeats! A lot of people his age would have disappeared from public life and retired on a rural estate somewhere. But not Lincoln. He went on to shepherd the American Civil War to a satisfactory conclusion and was in great part responsible for abolishing slavery in the country. He was so beloved that we still celebrate his birthday and display his face everywhere. Just think where this country would be if he had been consumed by despair that success wasn't coming quickly enough.

Thirty-five-year-old Elizabeth Thalhimer Smartt of Richmond, Virginia, isn't well-known like Abraham Lincoln, but her career as an author experienced a similar trajectory. Elizabeth was so sure that her book about her family's department store legacy would resonate with former shoppers all over the southern United States that she spent the better part of twelve years researching and writing it. There were, of course, sacrifices involved, especially the time she was able to devote to her husband and daughter and her independent branding consultancy. Elizabeth often questioned her decision, particularly after the book was finished and was not picked up by either an agent or a mainstream publisher. After waiting out a series of defeats, Elizabeth decided that if she didn't have faith in her book, no one else would. Working with a publisher that had connections to major distributors, Elizabeth released *Finding Thalhimers* to critical acclaim and superb regional sales and has been credited with reviving an important aspect of the South's retail history.

Cope with Setbacks

Of course, expecting some defeat and managing it effectively when it comes along are two different things. There are a few things you should remember about setbacks. First, they're temporary. In the moment, it may feel like you'll never get back on the horse, but that is certainly not the case. Most of my career setbacks have been dead and buried so long that I'd be hard put to remember all of them now. Second, they're usually isolated. Your setback now doesn't mean that you've failed in your career and probably doesn't say anything at all about your lifetime potential.

I think that the earlier you experience setbacks, the better off you are. Children with tough childhoods often become the most resilient adults because they learn at an early age that they won't die from most bad situations—they'll simply grow a harder shell. I've also noticed a certain immunity to minor setbacks that comes with age. As I've accumulated more experience in my career, the hurtful incidents that upset me so much that I'd lock myself in my bedroom with a carton of Ben & Jerry's (for example, my boss criticizing me, or losing a client) have become less and less damaging to my self-confidence. If something bothered me for two days when I was twenty-two, it would only bother me for two hours by the time I reached thirty-two.

In the midst of a defeat, simply ride things out as best you can. Feel the pain, but tell yourself that you've navigated the situation to the best of your ability and that things will turn around soon. Instead of sitting at home alone and torturing yourself, call a friend you haven't seen in a while and take in a funny movie. Pick up the hobby you've been neglecting for years and go to an event where you can meet like-minded people. When you're happy and you feel supported, your body will recover faster from the biological arousal of upsetting emotions. Make sure you get plenty of rest and exercise, and try to avoid substances that depress mood, like alcohol and caffeine. Give yourself a few weeks to feel better, and then resume progress on your goal.

Don't Let Your Goals Get the Best of You

Hopefully, by now you agree that well-defined goals can be the difference between success and mediocrity. But goal setting does have a dark side. The large-scale financial disasters of 2008 were in large part due to executives who blindly set and followed goals without paying attention to developments around them that should have prompted them to stop and think.

Sometimes setting a goal works so well that we become irrational and unethical in our attempts to achieve it. A classic example is the top-notch student who cheats on tests and plagiarizes term papers in order to maintain her straight-A average. In 1999, psychology researchers Christopher Chabris and Daniel Simons set out to investigate the phenomenon that goals can have a negative effect on performance. They told subjects to watch a video and count how many times the people in the clip passed a basketball among themselves. The subjects concentrated so intently on the goal that they failed to notice anything else taking place in the testing room—including when a woman in a gorilla suit took her place among the group! The bottom line? You'll get an edge by setting goals, for sure; just be aware of the potential pitfalls.

Now that you know that success won't happen overnight, you need a series of long-term goals in order to get to where you're meant to be. In this book I'm focusing on gaining an edge in the workplace, but your aspirations might include artistic, family, financial, physical, and public service goals. Spend some time thinking about the areas that are most important to you, and keep working until you have just a handful of goals to concentrate on. Please make sure these significant goals are truly your own, and not your partner's, family's, or employer's. The motivation to achieve won't be very strong or last very long if it's driven by someone else. Once you have your short list, use your goals to gain an edge by answering these questions:

- What exactly are you going to do, when, and how? For instance, it is better to say that you will attend three sales meetings this month than simply to remark that you plan to increase your knowledge of sales. Make sure you phrase the goal positively (instead of "Sacrifice my weekends to attend sales meetings," you could say "Make good use of my Saturdays this winter to master the mechanics of the sales process by March.")

- How should you determine if you have achieved your goal? How will you tell if you've made progress along the way? For example, you might say: "I will know that I am making progress toward my goal when I am able to complete the meeting exercises the other sales reps are responsible for."

- Is your goal something that you can realistically achieve in steps? While there should be a challenge inherent to the goal, you don't want the task to be so large or difficult that it destroys your motivation. Also, you don't want your success to be based on factors that are out of your control (such as the economy, the weather, or fate).

- Why is this goal important to your long-term success in this area? Will completion of the goal actually bring you closer to getting what you consider to be truly important in life?

- When are you going to start working on achieving your goal, and what is the deadline for completion? At what point should you stop and revisit your goal to make sure it's still a worthy exercise?

Did you write down your answers? Don't be lazy, because writing is half the battle. For even more of an impact, do as the successful Yale University students did. Turn the page and jot down some notes on your own strengths and weaknesses, obstacles you're likely to encounter, sacrifices you may have to make, knowledge you may need to acquire, and the people who can support you as you work to achieve your goals. Make your action plans for each goal short term so that your goals don't fall off the radar while you're coping with your boss's latest meltdown. And immediate to-do lists are a great idea, but don't let your Sharpie get too excited. Too many tasks on a checklist will either spread your attention too thin or cause you to feel so overwhelmed that you won't do anything.

No one experiences overnight success, but if you follow the lead of the individuals in this chapter, you'll be well on your way to great achievements. As Ed Viesturs did, periodically review your goals to ensure that you're on the right track and to determine if they need adjusting. And when you achieve a goal, don't just nod and smile and move on to the next big thing. It's important for your self-confidence and motivation that you celebrate the accomplishment and reward yourself for your hard work and dedication. Analyze what the experience taught you and what that means for future goal setting, and then call up your best friends for a night out on the town!

MYTHBUSTER'S SUMMARY

- There are very few—if any—genuine cases of overnight success. Most people try for a long time and experience several setbacks before achieving a high level of accomplishment.

- Few of us are just handed the ingredients for a fulfilling life. In most cases, if you want them for yourself you have to go out and grab them—and your surest path is by setting goals and following through on them.

- Theories abound on the best way to set goals, but research has most often supported the SMART approach of defining goals that are specific, measurable, achievable, relevant, and time-bound.

- Perseverance is defined as remaining constant to a purpose, idea, or task in spite of obstacles. Even if it doesn't come naturally to you, you can develop it through increased self-awareness and self-control and by training yourself to think positively.

- Don't expect your goals to be achieved in your ideal time frame. Be prepared to retool them as circumstances change, and expect to cope with some amount of defeat. When bad luck visits your goal, simply ride it out as best you can and resume progress when it makes sense.

Controversy Will Propel Your Career

lenty of people have made a good living on the back of controversy. After all, the phrase "any publicity is good publicity" became a cliché for a reason. The blogger who publicly denounces a high-profile celebrity will get a hundred comments in a matter of hours. The presenter who rants onstage at a televised award show will get more news attention than the actual winners.

Given the amount of noise in today's world, it's tempting to use controversy to draw attention to your message. But here's the problem. More often than not, controversial figures aren't respected. Human nature dictates that we can't look away from bad accidents or provocative tabloid reports, but does that mean you'd trust the driver or the people whose photos are splashed across the magazines in your grocery store? Just because you're paying attention to these people at the moment doesn't mean you want them in your life. And when it comes to people who court controversy, at what point does it seem totally insincere?

The reality is that being controversial generates attention for a little while, but it's usually not good for your career in the long term. You can take it from Jon and Kate Gosselin. Yeah, that's right, I'm going there: you know you want to hear the real story of what went down with these two!

On an Indian summer afternoon in October 1997, twenty-two-year-old Kate Kreider met twenty-one-year-old Jon Gosselin at a picnic. The nursing student and minister's daughter was immediately attracted to rich kid and hotel worker Jon, and less than two years later, they were married in a backyard wedding ceremony. Kate and Jon wanted kids right away, but Kate was diagnosed with polycystic ovary syndrome, so the couple began fertility treatments. In a space of time shorter than it takes most couples to get pregnant naturally, Kate conceived twins Cara and Madelyn via intrauterine insemination (IUI). The girls were born in October 2000.

Less than three years later, Jon and Kate were pining for "just one more" so they returned to the fertility clinic. In late 2003, Kate was being hospitalized for overstimulated ovaries when an ultrasound revealed that her latest round of IUI had produced seven fertilized embryos. Kate and Jon sobbed as the realization sank in that they were going to have seven more children to house, feed, and clothe. The couple couldn't support them—not even close—but because they were against selective reduction, they went ahead with the pregnancy. Though Kate was placed on bed rest for much of the next several months, miraculously healthy sextuplets Alexis, Hannah, Aaden, Collin, Leah, and Joel (one embryo did not develop on its own) were born in May 2004.

How much Jon and Kate did to seek out public attention for their unusual family is a matter of some debate. We know that both Kate's father's church and the state of Pennsylvania provided ample assistance in the form of a full-time nurse and baby furniture, food, and supplies. Jon launched a website, Sixgosse lins.com, and when the sextuplets were seventeen months old, the Gosselins were featured in a Discovery Health special titled *Surviving Sextuplets and Twins*. A second special a year later garnered good ratings, so the Gosselins were signed to a series—*Jon and Kate Plus 8*—that would air beginning in April 2007.

The little show, which was filmed three days a week, initially focused on Jon and Kate's struggles raising two sets of multiples and showed them doing mundane things the average family could relate to, like pumpkin picking and potty training. Jon and Kate were likable parents, and a small but loyal viewership rooted for them. *Jon and Kate Plus 8* eventually moved to its permanent home on cable network TLC and enjoyed modest success.

Gradually, though, Jon and Kate began to exhibit behavior on the show that turned off some of their fan base. Kate banned the beloved Aunt Jodi from their lives after a family squabble and ignored a painfully constipated Collin in favor of shopping for bedroom furniture. Their Christian values went out the window as the family grabbed as many free products, services, and lavish vacations from show sponsors as they could get their hands on.

When anti-Gosselin blogs sprang up criticizing Kate for her harsh treatment of Jon and the children, things went from bad to worse. It seemed that Jon and Kate relished the extra attention that went along with the controversy.

Rumors began to swirl about Jon and Kate's relationship in the spring of 2009. Tabloids reported that Jon was drinking with local college students and cheating on his wife, and that was when the media frenzy really started. TLC ran teasers for the fourth season's finale that speculated that Jon and Kate might be finished as a couple, and, not surprisingly, *Jon and Kate Plus 8*'s ratings went through the roof. More than 10 million viewers tuned in to see the announcement that Jon and Kate were separating, knocking out NBC, CBS, and Fox among women aged eighteen to thirty-four and setting records for a cable show.

Critics concerned about the children's exploitation called for TLC to stop the show as the elder Gosselins went through divorce proceedings, but Jon and Kate felt compelled to keep up the momentum. Jon seemed addicted to attention-seeking behavior, carousing with a different woman every week. For her part, Kate documented her family's every move on soundstages for *The Today Show* and *The View*. In a few short months, the twosome threw each other off mutual property, stole from each other, and hired lawyers to tear at the situation like rabid dogs.

Jon and Kate's behavior did keep the family in the public eye, but not in the way the parents hoped. Viewers quickly grew disgusted with Jon and Kate's antics and their obviously hypocritical claims that all they wanted was what was best for their children. Show ratings plummeted 80 percent, and first-run episodes in the fall of 2009 all had less than 2 million viewers. Still, the flashy

Kate capitalized on being on tabloid covers every week to pursue a television career of her own. She should have spent her time getting coached by professionals instead of airing her dirty laundry. Maybe then her guest-hosting gig on *The View* wouldn't have bombed as badly as it did, her talk show pilot with Paula Deen wouldn't have failed, and her spinoff series, *Kate Plus 8*, would have done better.

Both Jon's and Kate's emotional immaturity, demonstrated by the situations they created in order to be the center of attention, eventually left the public unwilling to support their activities any longer. They were painful proof that a career propelled by controversy is temporary and cannot be sustained.

As I talked about earlier, we're back to basics, and it is both possible and preferable to get noticed the old-fashioned way. In this chapter I'll cover how to be provocative without going overboard, how to be ethical, and how to generate visibility through the tried-and-true values of trust and assertiveness. I'll also address how to conduct yourself professionally in the wake of a scandal and how to resolve conflicts effectively so that you don't generate negative attention needlessly. Getting positive attention instead of negative attention, and being just famous instead of infamous, might take a little bit longer, but I promise it is well worth it in the end.

Be Provocative, but Not a Troll

Seth Godin, author of the popular business and marketing blog SethGodin.com, as well as bestselling books including *Tribes*, is someone whose thinking I admire a great deal. While this chapter was percolating in my brain, I decided to ask Godin his opinion on attention-seeking behavior. "People try to be controversial for two reasons," he says. "First, it works, and second, it feels safe, because once you get used to it, you can predict how it's going to play out. It's like starting a fight in a bar. All bar fights are essentially the same."

In the online world, the most common type of attention seeker is known as the troll. A troll's sole purpose in life is to stir up controversy with his inflammatory opinions. Trolls routinely put information out there that they know will rile the masses, promote themselves by indiscriminately bashing others' ideas, and call people names or disrespect them in other ways.

People might pay attention to trolls for a little while, but when the interest dies down, they're considered useless and irrelevant. As Godin says, "No one likes bar fighters or trolls, and sooner or later, we spend time with people we like. Bill O'Reilly doesn't have a lot of friends."

There's no doubt, though, that being provocative does get you noticed. So how can you do it tastefully? If you have an opinion that you feel passionately about, an opinion that's different from what the majority of people believe, then you should feel free to express it—as long as you can support it with a valid argument. While intelligent people may squirm a bit at controversy, they will usually appreciate a position that prompts them to think about and possibly reconsider their views. Your tone is critical too. When presenting a controversial matter, always be professional, and respond to detractors with diplomacy rather than defensiveness or self-righteousness.

When it comes to being provocative in the right way, online services such as Twitter and Facebook can be a blessing and a curse. Twitter, for instance, allows you to publish your thoughts in real time, and you should not abuse this privilege. Before you hit send, self-censor to make sure you're comfortable with the general public reading your message. Consider what each tweet says about your online brand, and how it might be perceived by managers, partners, and co-workers. On his blog, Six Pixels of Separation (www.twistimage.com/blog), Mitch Joel says that being provocative at all might not be the best way to generate business and validation. "It's worth your time to figure out and define your voice, and what you're trying to accomplish by taking part in these online social channels in the first place."

Of course, even if you do these things, there are still risks inherent to being provocative. Outspoken and confident people are sometimes looked upon as arrogant, and they tend to make enemies, especially if they come across in meetings and e-mails like they enjoy the sound of their own voices a little too much. And if the wrong person takes your message out of context or interprets it the wrong way, you'll have to clean up the mess quickly so that it doesn't permanently threaten your career.

If the contentious approach works for you, though, then you are probably wondering how to keep the flames alive. Can you hope to remain controversial throughout your entire career? Stuart Foster, who writes the Lost Jacket blog (http://thelostjacket .com), says no. "Trends shift, ideas come and go, and political and economic realities all play a role. Besides, the world at large wants you to fail and fall back to earth, because that would wipe the smug expression off your face," he comments.

The irony is that the people who are most successful at this often don't view themselves as provocative at all. "They are merely trying to establish themselves, solve problems in new and interesting ways, or let people know how passionate they are about the particular subject they are talking or writing about," says Foster. "And they maintain their creative brilliance by surrounding themselves with a great team, recognizing and seeking out their weaknesses and tempering some of their more controversial ideas."

Be Ethical

Seth Godin also shares that the most useful way to maintain visibility is to understand that you don't need the attention of everyone, just the people who matter. You'll earn this through behaving ethically.

Ethics is defined as the study of what is right and what is wrong. Similarly, an ethical issue requires a person to choose among actions that may be evaluated as right or wrong. In some situations, it's pretty obvious what the right and wrong thing to do is (for example, should I steal a bracelet from this store?), but often it's more unclear (for example, should I steal from a farm stand if I'm starving?). Unfortunately for those of us working in the business world, most of the ethical issues we'll face fall into the latter category.

Due to many high-profile corporate scandals, corporate ethics has been in the spotlight a good deal in recent years. Professional ethics, however, or ethics arising out of everyday work life, tends to involve issues that are more relevant to you as a midlevel or junior-level employee.

Ethical behavior on the job requires a certain mindset. You have a responsibility to act ethically, not because you might be caught doing something wrong, but because you feel it's necessary to do it right. This attitude sounds good in theory, but in times of workplace stress, it can go right out the window. Employees use all kinds of excuses for unethical behavior, including "Everyone does it this way," "I'm under so much pressure," "I have to get results," and "If I don't do it, someone else will, and then he'll get ahead and I won't."

The tendency to slip up starts in academic life, and few of us are able to say that we *never* cheated on a test or homework assignment in school. Yet most of us escaped unscathed. In the business world, however, the stakes can be much higher, especially now that several CEOs have been carted off to jail and everyone is paying more attention. Strong professional ethics involves more than just telling the truth or avoiding activities that are morally wrong. So what if you're not certain if an action is unethical? Here are some questions to ask yourself:

- Are there any potential legal restrictions or violations that could result from the action?

- Does my company have a code of ethics (formalized rules that describe what a company expects of employees) or a policy on the action?

- Would I like to see my action published on the front page of the *New York Times*?

- Will this action reflect badly on the company or on me personally?

- Will my action withstand open discussion with co-workers and managers and survive untarnished?

If you're still not sure, what else should you think about, or who can you ask for help?

- Consider that it's better to ask for permission than for forgiveness.

- Ask a proper authority such as your boss, a senior manager, a mentor, or the HR department:

  • Protect yourself by documenting the situation and recording critical details.

  • Be objective and factual to gain support.

- If things don't go well, be true to your moral code. At the end of the day, you have to answer to yourself!

Ethical issues in the workplace can be dicey, and as I've mentioned, proper solutions aren't always black and white. Here are a few examples of specific situations. Write your own answers and compare them to those provided below.

Question: A happy client sent an expensive thank-you gift to the office. My company doesn't have a policy about this, but the gift seems excessive and a little personal. Should I send it back?

_____

_____

_____

_____

_____

Answer: Not yet. Discuss the issue with your boss. If your boss agrees the gift is inappropriate and that you should return it, at least you won't be solely responsible if the client reacts badly. If your boss says to keep it, send a handwritten thank-you card and leave it at that.

Question: I am the entire IT department for a small firm. Our president believes some employees are spending too much time on the Internet doing non-work-related tasks and asked me to start monitoring employees' Internet usage without their knowledge. What should I do?

_____

_____

_____

_____

_____

Answer: Suggest that an acceptable Internet-use policy be developed with input from all. This action will raise everyone's awareness of the issue and serve as an implicit warning to some to change their Internet-related behavior.

Be Trustworthy

As a musician and producer, Andy Sharpe had the ideal skill set to found Song Division (www.songdivision.com), a company based in Australia and the United States that helps large groups tap into their creativity and experience the joy of songwriting. He recently told me a story about one of his team members, Monica.

"I bought Monica's team a flip camera so that she could capture video testimonials of happy clients just after they finished writing and recording their own songs," he says. "The first opportunity to use it was a big event for the Campbell Soup Company. I received a text from Monica immediately after the event. It said 'Huge success! The client loved it. But I forgot to get the testimonials and I'm kicking myself.'"

"Monica could have failed to tell me or offered a thousand excuses in order to deflect blame. But because the truth was laid out immediately, we were able to fix things so the same situation doesn't happen again. Now, we include 'get video testimonials' in event run sheets so it's part of the process and isn't missed."

Says Andy: "Honesty and trustworthiness are core values of ours. Although most people like to think they're honest, they often tell white lies to managers and clients here and there. But being trustworthy makes the business better on all levels. It means we make decisions based on hard facts and complete information, and everyone always knows where they stand. I look for team members who have the ability to tell the truth at all times. Making mistakes and communicating about them is how we keep growing as a business."

If every business were run like Song Division, perhaps we wouldn't be in such a difficult position today. In 2009, following the announcement of Bernard Madoff's $65 billion Ponzi scheme, the Edelman Trust Barometer study, an annual survey on business trust and credibility, saw trust among U.S. businesses drop an unprecedented 20 percentage points in just one year.

Stephen M. R. Covey is the son of legendary business thinker Stephen R. Covey and a bestselling author and successful entrepreneur in his own right. Covey defines trust as the confidence one instills in others based on character and competence. If you want to have a strong reputation at work, learning the skills associated with greater trust should be a top priority. In his book, *The Speed of Trust*, Covey defines the following thirteen behaviors as critical:

- **Talk straight.** Communicate clearly so that you cannot be misunderstood. Preface your discussions by declaring your intent, so you leave no doubt about what you are thinking. Don't manipulate people, distort facts, or leave false impressions.

- **Demonstrate respect.** Freely demonstrate fairness, kindness, and civility to all, regardless of what they can do for you.

- **Create transparency.** Be real and genuine and tell the truth in a way that people can verify. You can establish trust quickly by being open and authentic, erring on the side of disclosure, and having an open agenda.

- **Right wrongs.** Make restitution instead of just apologizing. Don't deny or justify wrongs because of ego and pride, and don't attempt to cover up mistakes.

- **Show loyalty.** Give credit to others and speak about people as though they are present. Don't disclose others' private information.

- **Deliver results.** Define your results up front. By establishing a track record, making the right things happen, being on time and on budget, and not making excuses, you quickly restore lost trust on the competence side.

- **Get better.** Continuously improve. Others will develop confidence in your ability to succeed in a rapidly changing environment. Don't be afraid to make mistakes, but learn from them. Develop formal and informal feedback systems and respond to them.

- **Confront reality.** Tackle the tough issues head-on. This facilitates open interaction and fast achievement, and it also allows you to engage the creativity, capability, and synergy of others in solving problems.

- **Clarify expectations.** Outline specifics up front. Always discuss and reveal expectations, and never assume they are clear or shared. Renegotiate if necessary, but don't violate expectations once they have been validated.

- **Practice accountability.** Hold yourself and others accountable. Don't avoid or shirk responsibility, and be clear on how you'll communicate progress.

- **Listen first.** Genuinely understand another person's thoughts and feelings before trying to diagnose or advise.

- **Keep commitments.** It is the quickest way to build trust in any relationship. Make keeping all promises the symbol of your honor.

- **Extend trust.** Be a trusting leader to those who have earned it. Don't extend false trust by giving people responsibility without the authority or resources to complete a task.

Be Assertive

Thirty-one-year-old Elizabeth Barry looks like a dancer, and the waiflike blonde from New York City has the talent to match. She spent her childhood in studios learning tap, jazz, ballet, and hip-hop. Elizabeth yearned to train at the University of the Arts in Philadelphia, but her father insisted she get a more solid education, so she settled for the tree-lined campus of the University of Massachusetts at Amherst and satisfied her passion through dance groups, theater productions, and classes.

When she graduated, the practical Elizabeth found the perfect way to make a good living immersing herself in the world she loved—she began working for dance magazines. As a former communications major, it surprised no one that Elizabeth was a naturally gifted salesperson. "I broke two company ad sales records and sold the most booth space for a trade show they hosted," she relates.

Soon, however, things turned sour. In traveling around the country to see her clients, many of which were mom-and-pop operations, Elizabeth learned that the expensive magazine space she was selling was resulting in poorly produced ads. "My clients were paying so much, and yet the ads looked thrown together, like an accountant had made them in Photoshop and sent them in," she said. "They just didn't know any better."

But Elizabeth was stuck. After all, her job was to sell, and she was doing that just fine. The situation nagged at her. "I knew my clients weren't getting the ROI to cover the ad buy most of the time, and then my superiors kept pushing me to sell to people who I knew wouldn't benefit." Then, one day, she knew she couldn't live with herself any longer. Elizabeth quit, and twelve days later she launched Elizabeth Barry and Associates, or EB&A (www .ebandassociates.com), a strategic marketing firm for dance organizations, in trendy Hoboken, New Jersey.

Learning from her past experiences, Elizabeth has made honesty and authenticity core aspects of her new business. She helps clients spend money wisely rather than frivolously, and the people who work with her trust her to do what's best for them. "It's better to do things the right way, without false pretenses, because when your clients get to the top and you've earned it, it feels amazing," she says. "Because we work so hard to make sure our work is high quality, nothing is more energizing than getting those e-mails that say 'I love it!'"

Hand-holding tends to have a negative connotation, but to small organizations in the dance industry, it's a valuable aspect of client service. "Most of my clients have had bad experiences in the past. They are used to pushy reps that yes them to death in order to make a sale," Elizabeth says. "But we'll tell them their ad or website needs work, and sometimes this means turning away their money so that we can help them get to where they need to be. When that happens, clients know they're in good hands, and they come back to us."

Elizabeth has built a dance marketing empire out of doing things differently. Over the years, she has added components to EB&A including an online magazine, *Gendance*. Because of her strong moral compass, Elizabeth feels comfortable charting unknown territory. "I'm young, pretty, and smart, and I'm bringing our industry online. Some people are threatened," she says, "but I know what I have to do. If I keep producing the best work, in time more people will follow me."

Elizabeth has mastered the art of assertiveness, which is commonly known as the ability to voice one's own opinions while respecting those of others. *Assertive* communication is nonaccusatory, nonjudgmental, and conversational in tone. Assertive communicators think before responding, avoid personalizing problems, and consider the big picture.

In contrast, *aggressive* communicators infer blame, place responsibility for a bad outcome on other people, and take unwarranted credit for successes.

Also in contrast is *passive* communication, which involves sharing information with reluctance, failing to offer feedback, and responding with blanket agreement.

Here are examples of the three types of communication in action:

- **The Scenario:** A co-worker asks you to do something outside your area of responsibility.

- **Aggressive response:** "So you think I'm junior level now, is that it?"

- **Passive response:** "Well . . . I guess I can" (then proceeding to ignore the request).

- **Assertive response:** "This isn't my area and I'm pretty busy, but let's work together to find a way to get it done."

- **The Scenario:** You meet your boss in her office after she insulted you publicly in a meeting.

- **Aggressive response:** "That was totally uncalled for."

- **Passive response:** "I heard there's leftover pizza in the kitchen" (pretending the meeting incident never happened).

- **Assertive response:** "I was a little taken aback by what you said in the meeting just now. Can you explain where you were coming from?"

- **The Scenario:** Your direct report forgot to complete a critical assignment and is now leaving the office.

- **Aggressive response:** "I see you're trying to escape without getting your work done."

- **Passive response:** "Don't worry about me, I'll just finish up myself."

- **Assertive response:** "I know you're on your way out, but this project needs to be done before the weekend. Is there any way I can help?"

Assertive people tend to run into fewer interpersonal snafus than other types of communicators, and they are also happier and more productive, whereas aggressive and passive people often alienate people and strain even their closest relationships. According to Elizabeth Scott, the stress management expert for About.com, answering the following questions will help you determine if you need to ratchet up your assertiveness quotient a bit.

- Do you have difficulty accepting constructive criticism? One sign is that you become easily upset and defensive when a comment is made about your performance. And saying "yes, but" to people who comment on your work.

- Do you find yourself saying yes to requests that you should really say no to, just to avoid disappointing people?

- Do you have trouble voicing a difference of opinion with others?

- Do people feel alienated when you do disagree with them?

- Do you feel attacked when someone has an opinion different from your own?

If you've answered yes to any of these questions, you might try to incorporate some assertive behaviors into your daily interactions. These might include:

- Telling a person you disagree with that you understand his point of view before making a contrary remark.

- Being consistent with your position, using facts to support it and an even tone of voice.

- Using "feeling" statements (for example, "I feel disappointed that you didn't tap me to work on your project") rather than accusatory statements (for example, "You don't trust me to work on your project").

- Striving for a compromise that benefits both parties.

One word of caution, though. Apparently, there is such a thing as being overassertive. In 2007 a research paper in the *Journal of Personality and Social Psychology*, published by the American Psychological Association, reported that organizational leaders who come across as either extremely low or extremely high in assertiveness were seen as least effective. In a series of studies, conducted by Daniel Ames of the Columbia Business School and Francis Flynn of the Stanford Graduate School of Business, workers were asked for their views of co-workers' leadership strengths and weaknesses.

The most common strengths noted weren't a surprise—traits like self-discipline and charisma made the list. However, the researchers were caught off guard when problems with assertiveness were listed as weaknesses. Ames commented, "Aspiring leaders who are low in assertiveness can't stand up for their interests, and they suffer by being ineffective at achieving goals and delivering results. On the other hand, people high in assertiveness are often insufferable. So, even though they may get their way, they're chocking off relationships with the people around them. As time goes by, the social costs add up and start to undermine the results. Most effective leaders push hard enough to get their way but not so hard that they can't get along." The bottom line: there's a happy medium, and if your co-workers don't have much to say about your level of assertiveness but you're still able to get things done and maintain good relationships, you're most likely doing all right!

Resolve Conflicts

Controversial and even assertive behavior in the workplace often leads to conflicts, some of which are unspoken. Unaddressed conflicts tend to result in personal dislike, a deterioration in teamwork, and a toxic work environment. Most people shy away from conflict, but knowing how to resolve it effectively will keep things running smoothly in your career and in your organization.

The first step is to identify your own style as well as the ones used in your team and/or organization. In the 1970s, Kenneth Thomas and Ralph Kilmann identified five main styles of dealing with conflict. They are:

- **Competitive:** Assertive and uncooperative, taking a power stance, and pursuing your own agenda at the other person's expense. The focus is on winning.

- **Accommodating:** Unassertive and cooperative, neglecting your own agenda to appease the other person, or yielding to the other person's point of view.

- **Avoiding:** Unassertive and uncooperative, sidestepping the issue, or refusing to deal with the conflict. May involve withdrawal from a threatening situation.

- **Collaborating:** Assertive and cooperative, understanding the needs and wants of the other person, and exploring the disagreement to find a mutually agreeable solution.

- **Compromising:** Moderately assertive and cooperative; involves "splitting the difference" between two positions so that both parties walk away somewhat satisfied.

Once you understand the style or styles being employed in your situation, you can use the following resolution process:

- **Get everyone on the same page.** Explain to the other parties your perception of the problem, and discuss the importance of solving it through concise collaboration rather than raw aggression.

- **Understand the nuances of the problem.** Lay out the reasons the problem must be addressed—for instance, is it negatively affecting the company's performance? Keep your observations objective and avoid attacking personalities.

- **Solicit opinions from all angles.** Ask the other parties involved about their viewpoints on the conflict and make sure each party's position is clear to the others.

- **Encourage open discussion.** Brainstorm potential solutions, ensuring that all parties have an opportunity to contribute.

- **Decide on a resolution.** Try to implement a solution that is satisfactory to all parties, even if positions are so different that it takes a little longer to unearth a compromise.

Surviving a Scandal

In the quiet seaside hamlet of Merrick, on New York's Long Island, Patrick Rodgers led a peaceful and comfortable existence. His active law practice handled criminal, corporate, family, and real estate cases. A notable member of the community since he was young, Patrick participated in the Merrick Kiwanis Club and the Merrick Chamber of Commerce and was elected president of the latter organization.

Then, Patrick's two brothers were diagnosed with cancer and

passed away within four months of each other. Blinded and confused by his grief, Patrick began to neglect his law practice. His clients filed complaints with the grievance committee, but Patrick simply ignored them.

One complaint in particular involved a divorce case in which Patrick missed a deadline and did not file the necessary papers, resulting in an adverse ruling against the client. "It is an attorney's duty to diligently and effectively represent a client in all matters that you are retained to undertake," Patrick explains. "I failed to uphold my end of the bargain when I was granted admission to the Bar, and hurt the law profession as a whole."

At the age of forty-three, Patrick was disbarred. "My mistake was that I did not get the help that I needed to deal with the mess I'd created," he says. "Even after the veil of my grief lifted, I was too stubborn."

Not only was Patrick out of a job, but he'd also sacrificed his professional reputation. It took him four hard years to regain his credibility and return to public service. "I received intensive training in mediation and discovered that it was my calling. I've finally made enough headway to pursue it."

Patrick can't change what happened in the past, but he strives to remember his mistakes and incorporate the values of honesty and trustworthiness into his job every day. "My status as a neutral party mandates that I'm authentic and able to reflect on my own shortcomings," he says. "It's going well, and I hope my story shows people that it's possible to survive a ruinous situation."

Those who court controversy are likely to find themselves embroiled in a scandal. This is obviously not a great thing to have happen, but if it does, all is not lost. Patrick isn't the only one who has managed to put scandal behind him. There are count-less examples in popular culture, including Bill Clinton, Martha Stewart, and more professional sports and entertainment figures than I have room to name here. When you're in the midst of a career-related scandal, the tendency might be to deny any wrong-doing and to feel anger at the person or people who exposed you. However, there are more productive ways to emerge from the ashes sooner rather than later. In their book, *Firing Back: How Great Leaders Rebound after Career Disasters*, Jeffrey Sonnenfeld and Andrew Ward offer these tips:

- **Fight not flight.** Face up to the reality of the situation. There are battles to restore your reputation and battles for revenge. Engage in the former and avoid the latter.

- **Rebuild heroic stature.** Provide a rational explanation of any injustice and express genuine contrition for any mistakes.

- **Prove your heroic mettle.** Regain trust by demonstrat-ing that the setback has not destroyed your professional expertise.

- **Discover a new heroic mission.** Don't define yourself by your past success or failure. Move on and show a new leadership vision.

It's also a good idea to focus on the areas of your life that haven't been affected by the scandal—for example, your hobbies or community involvement. As you strive to rebuild your career, continue to network inside and outside your organization and take on new projects that will restore your confidence. And finally, as Patrick demonstrated, it's critical to take stock of what went wrong and how you can prevent a similar outcome next time. Assessing the situation honestly and talking about your insights with close friends and family will put the scandal in its proper context and allow you to start anew without regret.

MYTHBUSTER'S SUMMARY

- Being controversial generates attention for a little while, but it's usually not good for your career in the long term.

- If you're going to be provocative, do it tastefully. Express views you feel passionately about, but make sure you can support them with valid arguments.

- The most useful way to maintain visibility is to understand that you don't need the attention of everyone, just the people who matter. You'll earn this through behaving ethically and generating trust.

- Instead of being controversial, be assertive: cultivate the ability to voice your opinions and resolve conflicts to your benefit while respecting the positions of others.

- Controversial or provocative individuals may find themselves mired in a career-related scandal. If this happens to you, take responsibility for restoring your reputation and learn from your mistakes so that you don't repeat them.

#3

Employers Want You to Be Yourself

Today's organizations do a terrific job with recruiting. In fact, they do such a good job that every new employee comes on board believing that the company is in desperate need of that individual and so everything that individual says and does will be appreciated and rewarded. Work in the business world for a while, though, and you'll notice that this is not entirely true, especially today, when an ultracompetitive job market means that employers can basically have anyone they want.

While today's employers do value the unique set of skills and experiences you bring to the table, they expect you to toe the line with respect to company conduct. You won't get away wearing ripped jeans to a client meeting because that's your personal style, and in a professional environment, you must learn to be politically sensitive and diplomatic even under difficult circumstances.

Alexandra Levit

Nicole Williams, author of *Girl on Top: Your Guide to Turning Dating Rules into Career Success*, agrees that employers don't necessarily want you to be yourself. "Companies value what makes you an individual, but—and this is a big but—as it applies to their current business situation," she says. "At the end of the day, most companies value people who are loyal, assimilate well, and use their individuality for the benefit of the company at large."

And what if you don't do this and insist on marching to the beat of your own drummer? In Nicole's opinion, it won't end well. "In my experience, the person who pulls attention, time, and energy away from the company, trying to drag it in a direction that is not consistent with the culture, will be undervalued and eventually dismissed—either literally or figuratively—as too much work," she says. "A company creates a spoken and/or unspoken code of conduct that is essential to operating smoothly. It's not always constructive or the best way of doing business, but in most instances there is a surprising resistance to doing it any other way, and frankly, the company's leaders who create or enforce the code don't appreciate being told to do it differently."

Twenty-six-year-old Jesse Monroe was determined to bring the technology industry's casual style to his new employer, a conservative start-up firm. "I'd worked in three technology companies since graduating from college, and across the board, people came to work wearing clean jeans and T-shirts," Jesse says. "Even though it was in the Deep South, I still thought my new company would be the same deal. After all, it was a software manufacturer!" But when Jesse showed up to work in his usual ensemble, his managers, decked out in business casual, did not appreciate it.

"They said that my dress showed a lack of respect—not really something I wanted to hear and completely untrue in my opinion."

Jesse responded by showing his managers pictures of employees on the job at hot tech companies like Microsoft and Google. "It was important to me to be allowed to dress in clothing I felt comfortable in, so I thought I could make a case that we could dress down and still be successful in the marketplace." His primary manager's response, however, was this: if Jesse enjoyed the Google culture so much, maybe he should work there. "I didn't get fired and eventually agreed to buy some new clothes, but from that point on, I felt they resented me a little for suggesting we change things," he says.

In this chapter I'll talk through ways that "being yourself" could be detrimental to your potential within an organization. I'll start by defining what it means to be professional in the workplace, including the proper way to dress, converse, and behave. Then I'll explore the common problem of overexpressing the very traits you were hired for—taking initiative, managing change, and talking straight.

What It Means to Be a "Professional"

When it comes to nebulous terms, I like Wikipedia definitions because if something is on Wikipedia, it usually means that thousands of people have looked at the content and can't find anything to argue about. So I turned to Wikipedia to find a modern definition of a professional and found this: "A professional is a member of a vocation founded upon specialized educational training. In western nations such as the United States, the term commonly describes highly educated, mostly salaried workers, who enjoy considerable work autonomy, a comfortable salary, and are commonly engaged in creative and intellectually challenging work. Because of the personal and confidential nature of many professional services and thus the necessity to place a great deal of trust in them, most professionals are held up to strict ethical and moral regulations."

To me, this definition means that professionals get a lot of freedom and perks, and in exchange they are held to high standards of behavior and appearance. In my first book, *They Don't Teach Corporate in College*, I suggest that the best way to be professional is to develop a strong corporate persona. By corporate persona, I mean the mature, professional, and competent face you project to the work world. It doesn't matter if you're really an introvert who prefers to play video games all night or if you've been known to drink your older (and larger) brother under the table at a family wedding. You can still have a corporate persona that positively influences people's perceptions of you so that you will be successful in the business environment. My favorite example of someone with an exceptional corporate persona is Oprah Winfrey. The little that is known about Oprah's personal life indicates that she hasn't necessarily had the easiest time of it (she was abused as a child, she struggles constantly with her weight, she could never get that Stedman guy to marry her), but watching her show over the course of twenty years, you'd never see an Oprah who was anything less than completely polished, friendly, and concerned with the best interests of her audience. Even if Oprah woke up that morning ten pounds heavier or was mad because she'd learned a guest had lied about writing a memoir she recommended, you never see her lose her cool. Oprah knows she has a brand to uphold, an expectation she must live up to, and she doesn't let her guard down, even for a moment.

If your goal is to get beyond middle management, then being unique isn't going to cut it. It may be a hard pill to swallow, but sometimes trying to be too much of an individual implies that you're not willing to be a team player and adhere to rules that the rest of your colleagues have agreed to follow. Instead of just showing up and being yourself, you're going to need to display a better-dressed, better-behaved, and more diplomatic version of yourself. Let's start with the thing that's easiest to change—your appearance.

Dressing Up—and Down—at Work

Lawrence Polsky is a boy from the heart of New York, so when he decided to grow his hair a little long in his midthirties, he didn't think it was anything to worry about. But one day, Lawrence's boss called him into the office and said that the president of the company had requested that he cut his hair. "I couldn't believe that the president would waste his time commenting on my hair, especially since I dressed nicely and did my job well, but there it was. It was a message that I couldn't be myself," he says.

Most people who have been in the business world a while understand the real no-nos when it comes to workplace dress— no halter tops, no flip-flops, no ripped T-shirts, no baseball caps—you get the picture. But as Lawrence's story shows, other aspects of our appearance are sometimes critiqued as well, and determining the most appropriate look for business and business-casual environments is a little more complicated. Naturally, the first thing you should do is look around. You should aim to look exactly like the people at the level above you, because this will enable your co-workers and managers to see you in that position. If you regularly meet with clients, then your wardrobe should match that of your most conservative customer. Your goal should be classic and consistent. It's great to incorporate a trendy piece now and then, but don't go overboard expressing your personal style.

The traditional staple of the business-casual wardrobe for women is the pantsuit in a neutral shade—black, brown, navy, or gray. I also like the look of tailored black pants with a crisp white shirt or light sweater. If you're into skirts, please don't wear anything that cuts your thighs in half. Choose a simple sheath with a casual blazer or cardigan instead. When judging your appearance, others will most often look at your jewelry and your footwear, so invest in a handful of high-quality gold and silver pieces and two or three pairs of stylish but comfortable shoes. Keep your accessories—and your makeup—to a minimum.

Men working in a business-casual environment should stick to sports coats and button-down shirts paired with neatly pressed khaki, wool, or linen pants. Select understated colors like brown or maroon, and if you're going to wear a tie, avoid obnoxiously loud prints. If you appear at work with your face clean-shaven and your hair an acceptable length (thank you, Lawrence) and unscuffed oxfords or loafers on your feet, you should be good to go. In a BNET article, "Five Rules of Style for the Business-Casual Workplace," corporate style consultant Anthea Tolomei offers writer Christian Chensvold a great litmus test to tell at a glance if a garment is really work-worthy: the detergent test. If you can wash it at home, it's probably not business wear.

If you work in a jeans culture like the tech companies described earlier, good for you, but that doesn't automatically mean no one is paying attention to how you look. Your jeans should be clean and free of holes, and they should fit appropriately. On the opposite side of the spectrum, formal business attire should be reserved for those environments that encourage it. If you're the only one in the office dressed to the nines, your co-workers may perceive you as stuffy and elitist. In offices where everyone looks like Barney Stinson from *How I Met Your Mother*, though, you'll want to compete with the best of them. Both men and women should consider employing a tailor to make a custom suit.

Admittedly, this is no small undertaking. After identifying a tailor near you through the Custom Tailors and Designers Association (www.ctda.com), you can expect to visit with him at least twice for consultations and fittings. And then there's the price. According to the BNET article, men's custom-tailored suits can run anywhere from just under $1,000 for a basic handmade two-piece in Asia to $25,000 for the full, perfectly fitted three-piece monty made by the finest tailors. The median range is between $2,500 and $5,000. Plus, you'll want to show off your custom suit with a nicely fitted shirt, a complementary silk or linen pocket square, high-quality socks, and a pair of dress shoes.

On the bright side, these suits last forever if taken care of properly, and such a look will do wonders for your reputation.

Think First, Communicate Second

When it comes to conversation topics at work, talking about whatever comes to mind may not necessarily be appreciated, and it could actually compromise your reputation. In general, I suggest avoiding any discussion involving sex, drugs, or politics, because even if you are sure all of your co-workers are on the same page as you, you're probably wrong about *someone*. Gossip is another thing to watch out for. Please don't repeat with relish anything that could be hurtful or damaging to a co-worker, and for the love of God, don't be the person who originates the gossip. If someone shares a juicy tidbit, simply nod and smile.

Seemingly inoffensive information can actually get you into trouble, so before you open your mouth, think about whether the listener really needs to hear what you're about to say and how he will react to it. John Olson, for example, was an assistant manager at Publix Supermarkets in Florida, a workplace filled with golf-playing fanatics. John, on the other hand, preferred to spend his time off in more adventurous pursuits. Once, he took an airboat into the Everglades and spent the afternoon wrestling alligators, and when John's boss asked him how he'd spent his day, John told him the truth. Unexpectedly, John's manager flew into a breathless rant about how John was an irresponsible manager and was setting a poor example for his hourly employees. So, you never know.

According to Anthony Balderrama in his CareerBuilder.com article "13 Things to Keep to Yourself at Work," other conversation topics to steer clear of include:

- Your medical history

- Your religion

- Your life of privilege and how you spend your abundance of money

- Your emotional issues and/or therapy sessions

- Your compensation details or other confidential HR issues

- Your job search or future work plans

- Your personal life, including your love affairs and sexual orientation

This last one may be the most controversial, since there are many people who believe that all homosexual individuals should be able to be "out" at work. When I covered this issue in the *Wall Street Journal*, the piece received the most comments of any column I wrote this year. Now, I'm not going to tell people how to live their lives, but I would like to encourage people to use caution when their career could be at stake. Allow me to share Bob Johnson's story.

A few years ago, Bob interviewed for a marketing and communications position with the Lebanese American University, a university chartered in New York with campuses in Lebanon. "I did have some reservations about working for LAU," he remembers. "It didn't have an equal opportunity employer notice on its website or job ad. When I interviewed for the position, LAU did not ask about my sexual orientation, nor did I volunteer it. I got the job, and I took it, thinking it would be an adventure."

Through the course of Bob's tenure at LAU, which included listening to a speech from the Iranian president that panned homosexuality and traveling to the deeply closeted city of Beirut, Bob learned that openness about his sexuality would not be tolerated. Despite his discretion, though, Bob received a forty-five-day performance improvement plan from his manager outlining deficiencies in his work performance. Exactly forty-five days later, LAU fired him. "It didn't make any sense. I performed all of the tasks that my job required and more," he says. "So months later, I discussed my confusion with a co-worker, who looked at me and said, 'Bob, they didn't fire you because of job performance.'"

Don't get me wrong—rights protections for the lesbian, gay, bisexual, and transgender community have come a long way. As of the writing of this book, sixteen states have laws that protect LGBT individuals from job discrimination. However, there is currently no federal law that safeguards people from being fired because they are gay, so think before you open that door.

Since written communication is as important as verbal communication, you should definitely watch your trigger finger with respect to e-mail. In general, if you need to discuss a complicated issue or to impart negative sentiment, e-mail is not the best vehicle. If you must communicate this way, make sure you are as concise as possible, use a meaningful subject line, and summarize your key points at the very top of the message. Use spell-check and reread every e-mail twice before sending it, as it's not uncommon to get caught up in the heat of the moment and say something you later regret. Don't send e-mail to work contacts that's irrelevant to your business, and don't type in all caps or use cutesy emoticons or acronyms, such as ROTFL. You have to assume that every e-communication could be read by a nosy IT administrator, or worse, the CEO.

Indeed, most of the e-mail snafus that occur in business settings arise because a message falls into the wrong hands. In this respect, the "Reply to All" and "Blind CC" features are real troublemakers. Please use the "Reply to All" function very sparingly, and read the name of every intended recipient before sending your message. As for "Blind CC," remember that the blind part only works for the first message sent. If someone who was a blind copy recipient replies to all, all of the contacts on the message will see who was blinded—a circumstance that could have political fallout. Two final e-mail tips: make certain that you read a message's entire string before adding new people to the distribution list; and in the process of adding people, look over the "To" field to ensure that your e-mail program didn't auto-fill a name incorrectly. At least five times in my career, I've received e-mails intended for another Alexandra, and sometimes they contained confidential information. Don't let this sending error happen to you.

The online world is another place where "being yourself" could be hazardous to your health at work. The blurring of the personal/professional line starts when people are in school. A 2009 study published in the *Journal of the American Medical Association* found that 60 percent of medical schools reported an incident of a student posting inappropriate content. "Nearly 100 percent of students ages 22–26 post information that's deemed unprofessional, uses profanity or features intoxication," says Jeanne Farnan, an assistant professor at the University of Chicago's Pritzker School of Medicine, in an article for Medill News Service. The problem was so severe among these medical students—who are supposed to adhere to a stricter moral code than other young professionals—that the school created a training initiative designed to help students manage the interface between professionalism and digital media.

So how should people in the business world manage their online presence? The first thing you should do is perform a Google search on yourself. This is so important that I'm going to ask you to do it right now. Write down what you see in the first three pages of search results here:

_____

_____

_____

_____

If you don't like something you found or you discover that the bulk of information pertains to someone else with the same name, beef up your own online offerings and submit guest blog posts and articles that showcase your professional expertise so that these items appear first instead of that embarrassing article about your neighbor suing you. Professional help with this issue is available via search engine marketing firms like Defend My Name (www.defendmyname.com), which use labor-intensive linking strategies to push undesirable items off the first several pages of the major search engines.

When it comes to social network use, any information that you wouldn't be comfortable showing to your grandmother or religious officiant should really be off-limits, because you can never be sure who might be able to gain access without your permission. However, creating boundaries between social networks allows you to post personal information and photos without worrying that you've shared too much with managers or direct reports. For example, some people have chosen to use Facebook.com for family and friends, and they reserve LinkedIn.com for business contacts. Note that you don't have to be friends with the world on every social network, you can use different levels of privacy settings for different networks, and you don't have to import status updates and news items to every network. My recommendation is to simply make clear to your contacts what you are using the various networks for. If a colleague asks to be your Facebook friend but you are using Facebook exclusively to keep up with your college buddies, just tell her so politely and invite her to connect on LinkedIn. Being honest up front very well may save you from an awkward situation later.

Business world employees rely heavily on online communication to get work done, and there is no longer a generational discrepancy here. When it comes to being online at work, don't surf during in-person meetings or type when people in virtual meetings can see or hear you. If you're part of an instant-message culture, there's nothing wrong with periodic conversations via IM, but don't get into the habit of messaging people every five minutes, because no one's going to get any work done that way, and don't gossip via IM, because an IT guy could be watching. Finally, post status updates on company time sparingly, unless of course it's your job to do so. If your boss sees that you've tweeted twelve times in a business day, she's going to wonder what she's paying you for. Bottom line: be cognizant that online communication is always monitored in some respect, so it's not a place to fully be yourself.

Sit Down, You're Rocking the Boat

When I was a little girl, my grandfather told me that when his parents arrived at Ellis Island, our name was changed to "Levit" from something much more Russian and exotic. You've probably heard the same story. Your immigrant relatives didn't speak English, so the clerk on duty either misunderstood the name or decided that it was too complicated. According to genealogist Donna Przecha, that's not exactly how it happened, because the clerks at Ellis Island didn't write down names. Rather, they worked from lists that were created by the shipping companies. Emigrants bought ship passage at offices near their homes, and because sellers typically spoke the same language as the emigrants, names were transcribed correctly. Many emigrants changed their names on purpose before leaving their homelands.

Why would they do this? Well, the desire to assimilate is a strong one, and most new immigrants wanted to become true Americans as quickly as possible, so they selected American-sounding names. They also knew that the faster they assimilated, the better luck they'd have finding employment. After all, there was no such thing as sensitivity training in the workplace of the late nineteenth and early twentieth centuries, and employers made no secret of the fact that they found foreign names difficult and preferred their workers to be Americanized.

One hundred years later, Darwin Stephenson of Casper, Wyoming, was a young vice president at a physical labor logistics company. Overseeing a $70 million territory, Darwin felt he was a good ten years underqualified for the job, but his employer thought he had potential and would rise to the occasion. It was the promotion of a lifetime, and Darwin took on the challenge of turning around a fledgling division and motivating hundreds of blue collar, unionized workers who had stopped caring about their jobs. "My approach was to break down cultural barriers between workers and management by being approachable, caring and visible," he says.

Good as it sounds, Darwin's strategy didn't work. His "regular guy" attitude didn't fly with the employees, who perceived him as insincere and fake, and his efforts to become a different type of leader fell flat. The old-timer leaders didn't like Darwin either. "They had become quite comfortable with the status quo, and my attempts to improve things just seemed like more work," he says. "My predecessor had used fear tactics to keep everyone in line, and management saw my down-to-earth approach as a vulnerability in a very risk-averse culture." In less than a year, both employees and managers alike were gunning for Darwin's demise. He was terminated without cause shortly thereafter.

Talented as Darwin was, he failed in his role due to an inability to assimilate into his corporate culture. To avoid making the same mistake, whether you are in a new organization or a new position, you should lie low as you take the time to study your environment. Make note of the political landscape and how people interact within it, and watch for the spoken and unspoken rules of engagement. Look at everything from how people dress for the holiday party to the language that's emphasized in the annual report, and watch the most successful individuals for clues as to how you should appear and behave. "To assimilate effectively, you want to identify what the company values most, and follow that lead," says author and workplace expert Nicole Williams. "You want to ask yourself: How do people treat and communicate with one another? How are ideas and information shared (or not)? How do company leaders treat their own people, customers, and vendors? What time do they show up and leave every day? In one of my first jobs, for example, I observed that the most influential person in the company came in at seven a.m., and if you also arrived at the crack of dawn, he would share vital information, believing you were a part of his 'early morning team.' It was a critical part of being successful in that company."

Even if you were hired as a so-called change agent, don't expect to swoop in and transform your organization overnight. There's a reason why 70 percent of change initiatives fail, so get to know how and why things are done a certain way before you take a torch to them. While it's true that you must prove your value, it doesn't hurt to start small. Gain gradual buy-in for your ideas by sharing them with your manager first, and then, one team at a time. Pay attention to any resistance you're encountering, and cope with it as it comes up rather than allowing it to fester.

You were brought in because of your unique combination of

skills and expertise, so you should use them to improve the company's lot, but stubbornly forcing yourself on people isn't going to get the job done. Even if the dysfunctional, ineffective nature of your workplace has you stifling screams of frustration, you must be able to express your opinions from the perspective of someone who fits in and is a respected team member. More about that in the next section.

How to Be Diplomatic

Forty-one-year-old Rob Bedell isn't really from anywhere. He was born in New York, raised in Arizona, and educated at Loyola Marymount University in Los Angeles. Like Darwin Stephenson, Rob was once a rising star. "I worked for a weekly newspaper group for many years, starting as a regular grunt in the classified sales department," he says. "My management saw that I had promise, and they promoted me to manager."

Except Rob had a problem. He didn't respect his boss. "He got into his position because he inherited it, not because of his sales or interpersonal skills," Rob remembers. "He ruled with an iron fist, and it wasn't motivating our staff. I decided to tell him my concerns, and admittedly, I didn't set the conversation up properly. Instead of trying to find out more about why he was doing things this way, I criticized him and he got defensive."

Rob's relationship with his boss continued to deteriorate, and then one evening, his mother was in a car accident. She wasn't injured, but Rob had to deal with the fallout and e-mailed his boss to say that he would be in late. Rob's manager alerted the rest of the staff by e-mail, adding snidely that he didn't understand why Rob was missing work since his mother was all right.

Rob forwarded his boss's message to the organization's top dog, the publisher. "I said that I thought my boss's e-mail was completely inappropriate, and that perhaps he would have preferred if my mother was seriously hurt," he says. "My boss found out and barged into my office, accusing me of trying to get him fired. I told him that he was handling that quite well all by himself."

Rob's lack of diplomacy turned an already difficult situation into an intolerable one. Even though his boss was partly in the wrong, Rob didn't do himself or his staff any favors by provoking him. The truth is, there are always going to be people you don't like at work. What separates successful careerists from lackluster ones is the ability to get along despite inevitable personality clashes.

The hallmark of the diplomatic person is assertiveness, or readily expressing your views while respecting the opinions and dignity of others. Diplomatic people recognize that they are most likely to get their own needs met if they can communicate their goals without evoking hostility in the other party. They are tactful, which means they have the ability to get across potentially hurtful information to another person without offending her. These are the individuals who can come out of necessary and frank conversations with their reputation intact. Let's look at how they do it:

- **They approach negotiations from a win-win perspective.** In his book *The 7 Habits of Highly Effective People*, Stephen

R. Covey says that if you want another person to cooperate with you, first analyze what he wants and then communicate how working with you can help him get it (i.e., you win, and the other person wins).

- **They seek to solve problems rather than spar.** Diplomatic individuals lay out the scenario calmly and solicit the other person's help in finding the best solution. They listen carefully to the other person's feedback without interrupting and they ask questions for clarification.

- **They are tolerant of opposing points of view.** Diplomatic employees respect that they may not always see eye to eye with other people, so they don't waste time and energy forming judgments about their co-workers. In conversations in which a fundamental difference of opinion is at play, they use facts to support their ideas and use nonaccusatory language such as "I think that . . ." or "It seems that . . ." rather than "You think that . . ." or "You always . . ."

- **They use positive body language.** Diplomatic people maintain an even, audible tone when they speak. They relax their body and keep an appropriate distance away from the people with whom they're conversing. They always make eye contact.

Of course, you can control your own behavior, but you can't control other people's, so you must be prepared to react professionally when someone attacks you. The key is not to let yourself get angry or upset, because goading you into a shouting match is exactly what the other person wants. Instead, stay calm, hear the person out, and be empathetic to her point of view. If she says hurtful things you know she doesn't mean, try not to take them personally, for you may not understand where these comments are truly coming from. Can't keep from losing your cool? Pay attention to the signs that you're about to blow (hands shaking, tears pricking at your eyes, etc.). Then politely excuse yourself and say you'll talk to the person another time. If you're on the phone, it's even easier. Just say that you need to take an urgent call and request a follow-up conversation later that day. Your efforts at diplomacy will be much more effective after you've both had a chance to cool down.

It also helps to be proactive. If you know there is a particular situation that gets to you, practice how you will respond the next time it rears its ugly head. And if you find a specific person difficult to deal with on a regular basis, schedule a lunch or a meeting and ask him frankly how the two of you can work better together. A compromise or a sacrifice might be necessary, but being perceived as the bigger person can only help your reputation in the office at large.

Honesty Is Not Always the Best Policy

After graduating from the University of Massachusetts at Amherst, Angela Lussier worked in a series of industries, from social science research to manufacturing, and in each position she felt stifled. In one position in particular, Angela, then twenty-eight, thought she was going to lose her mind. Even though no clients ever visited her office, she'd gotten in trouble for wearing sneakers instead of heels due to a foot injury and for failing to close a deal after her boss had sabotaged her in the meeting.

When it came time to fill out the annual employee evaluations, Angela decided to be completely honest. "Management said they wanted to know what we were thinking, that this was an ISO 9001 certified company that was committed to continuous improvement," she says. "So I critiqued the management style and the lack of autonomy and trust, the fact that if we wanted to leave the office for any reason we were treated like grounded teenagers, and the fact that inconsistent demands from different managers often set us up for failure."

The evaluation was not anonymous, and Angela was called out by her boss as being insubordinate. "From that point on, I was viewed as a rebel who was acting up and needed to be contained," she says.

I hope this story speaks for itself. Like Angela, you might be tempted to use company evaluations, your own performance reviews, or others' performance reviews to express your true opinions about the organization or its people. I urge you to use discretion, because blatant honesty—especially when your feedback is negative—is another way that "being yourself" can wreck havoc on your career. Even if a survey is technically anonymous, it can often be traced to you anyway (one sneaky way companies do it is by providing each employee with a unique URL) and your candidness could come back to haunt you. Employers may say that they value your opinion, but the hard truth is, more often than not they simply want you to tell them how great things are. If you genuinely feel that your organizational culture is one that supports growth and change and that you can share criticism without being penalized for it, then make sure you are unwaveringly constructive in your comments. Read over your feedback twice or three times to ensure that everything you say is motivated by your concern for the company, not concern for yourself.

Even if you're leaving the company and are in the midst of an exit interview, you should dial it down. After all, what do you have to gain by airing all your grievances now? Having the last word is not a good enough reason to risk ruining the good reputation you built with that company, or to close the door on any opportunities to work with that organization in the future.

When it comes to the inherent danger of "being yourself" at work, Nicole Williams has these parting words: "Put yourself in your employer's shoes, and you'll see that viewing employees as individuals can actually be threatening," she says. "Many companies talk a good game about individuality and innovation when, in fact, change means discomfort, dissention, and even danger. You have to know what's important to you and what's important to the company, and then focus on the overlap. When you encounter a disconnect, explore it gently with people you know and trust to see if it's a battle worth fighting."

MYTHBUSTER'S SUMMARY

- While employers value the unique set of skills and experiences you bring to the table, they expect you to toe the line with respect to company conduct.

- In determining the most appropriate look for your business or business-casual environment, you should aim to look exactly like the people at the level above you, because this will enable your co-workers and managers to more easily see you in that position.

- Before you open your mouth, think about whether the listener really needs to hear what you're about to say, and how he will react to it. Even if you are sure all of your co-workers are on the same page, you're probably wrong about *someone*.

- Gain gradual buy-in for your ideas by sharing them with your manager first, and then, one team at a time. Pay attention to any resistance you're encountering, and cope with it as it comes up rather than allowing it to fester.

- The hallmark of the diplomatic person is assertiveness, or readily expressing your views while respecting the opinions and dignity of others. Diplomatic people recognize that they are most likely to get their own needs met if they can communicate their goals without evoking hostility in the other party.

MYTH
#4

Being Good at Your Job Trumps Everything

My friend Louie is an exceptional piano player. He has been playing by ear since the age of three, and he can perform anything from Schubert to the Arctic Monkeys flawlessly after hearing a song just once. Everyone who listens to him says that Louie is one of the most gifted musicians they've ever come across. The only trouble is, not that many people hear him, because Louie sits in his Queens apartment and waits for the phone to ring. No matter how many times I lecture him about the importance of promoting his piano playing on the New York music scene, Louie feels that he's good enough for producers to come to him. And usually, they don't.

Louie adheres to the popular myth that being good at your job trumps everything else—that you will attract attention, recognition, and opportunities through sheer quality alone. And this myth is no truer for you than it is for Louie. The reality is that you can be the most talented employee your company has ever hired, but if your contributions aren't visible and people don't value what you do, it simply won't matter. Admittedly, this is a tough concept to get your head around. Chances are that you spent sixteen or more years of school believing that achievement was something you kept to yourself. Sharing your good grades was considered rude, and being an A student carried you far whether people knew you were smart or not.

In business, this is not so. "I've known lots of people who were very good at their jobs but didn't understand the importance of schmoozing certain people in the organization," says Leslie Singer, cofounder and creative director of branding shop HS Dominion (www.hsdominion.com). "They myopically focused on their individual roles and thought that if they came in every day and did their jobs, that would suffice. They didn't get that they were part of a village." If this sounds familiar, don't feel too bad. I'm right there with you. In my first job, I focused on doing stellar work and rarely left my cube. Imagine my surprise when the girl who had started at the same time as me, who flitted around the office chatting with everyone and barely contributed anything, got promoted ahead of me. When a position opened up, she snagged it because people knew who she was and liked her. The only people who knew me were my immediate boss and the colleague from another department with whom I ate lunch, and I lost out.

I'm not too familiar with the New Testament of the Bible. But occasionally a friend will point me to a section that's relevant to the challenges we face in business, such as this one from Matthew 25:14–29 called the Parable of the Talents:

A man traveling into a far country called his own servants and delivered unto them his goods. And unto one he gave five talents, to another two, and to another one; to every man according to his several ability; and straightway took his journey. Then he that had received the five talents went and traded with the same, and made them other five talents. And likewise he that had received two, he also gained other two. But he that had received one went and digged in the earth, and hid his lord's money.

After a long time the lord of those servants cometh, and reckoneth with them. And so he that had received five talents came and brought other five talents, saying, "Lord, thou deliveredst unto me five talents: behold, I have gained beside them five talents more."

His lord said unto him, "Well done, thou good and faithful servant: thou hast been faithful over a few things, I will make thee ruler over many things: enter thou into the joy of thy lord."

He also that had received two talents came and said, "Lord, thou deliveredst unto me two talents: behold, I have gained two other talents beside them."

His lord said unto him, "Well done, good and faithful servant; thou hast been faithful over a few things, I will make thee ruler over many things: enter thou into the joy of thy lord."

Then he which had received the one talent came and said, "Lord, I knew thee that thou art an hard man, reaping where thou hast not sown, and gathering where thou hast not strawed. And I was afraid, and went and hid thy talent in the earth; lo, there thou hast that is thine."

His lord answered and said unto him, "Thou wicked and slothful servant, thou knewest that I reap where I sowed not, and gather where I have not strawed. Thou oughtest therefore to have put my money to the exchangers, and then at my coming I should have received mine own with usury.

"Take therefore the talent from him, and give it unto him which hath ten talents. For unto every one that hath shall be given, and he shall have abundance: but from him that hath not shall be taken away even that which he hath."

The story makes the point that it doesn't matter what we're given—it's what we do with it that matters. Some of us are born with or are given more gifts than others, but this doesn't necessarily mean we'll be compensated for them. Instead, we have to take those gifts into the world and multiply our accomplishments.

We used to live in a time where you could do your job well and count on a promotion every few years, but unfortunately that's no longer the case. Today, rewards and recognition are scarce commodities, and in order to snag them, you must be calculated and thoughtful in presenting your accomplishments. This chapter will advise you on how you can promote yourself effectively so that your excellent work receives the attention it deserves. I'll start by discussing why knowledge isn't power and why popular people are considered to be better performers. Next I'll talk about quantifying your contributions and appropriately alerting others to your successes. Communication is critical here too, so I'll spend some time addressing how to get noticed by your boss and executives, how to be a spokesperson for your organization, and how to create an online brand that showcases your best work.

Why Knowledge Isn't Power

Do you know where the phrase "knowledge is power" comes from? It was coined by British statesman, essayist, and philosopher Sir Francis Bacon in the sixteenth century. Back then, the average person didn't know a lot—we come across more information in one day now than some of them did in their entire lives! Knowledge was a hot commodity. "I personally think that the 'knowledge is power' belief started with the invention of the Gutenberg press," says Leanne Hoagland-Smith, author of *Be the Red Jacket in a Sea of Gray Suits* (www.processspecialist.com). "The technological advances after this, including the invention of nuclear energy and the space race, led this belief to become the mantra for formal learning. Knowledge was perceived as the be-all, end-all."

Today, however, there's no shortage of knowledge to be gleaned, and how we get access to it has changed drastically in the last ten years. When I was in high school, for example, I had to go to the library if I wanted to research a paper. But students in 2011 can simply log on to the Internet and get the sources they need in seconds. Procuring the information is the easy part. But doing something with it? That's the true challenge. Denis Kristanda, author of the Investing by Me website (http://investingbyme

.com), agrees. "As long as you don't convert your knowledge into action, that knowledge will not become power," he says. "Let's say that you have knowledge about making money from the stock market. Without taking the action to open an account and make a trade, your knowledge is just simply knowledge and nothing more. But once action is taken, that knowledge gains power. You start making money and getting more market experience."

The relationship between knowledge and power was studied by Daniel Sarewitz, director of the Consortium for Science, Policy, and Outcomes at Arizona State University, and his research partner Richard Nelson, a professor of economics and innovation at Columbia University. Sarewitz and Nelson looked at the concept of human know-how, which puts knowledge to work in the real world. Reports Denise Caruso in her *New York Times* article "Knowledge Is Power Only If You Know How to Use It," "Know-how is how scientific discoveries become routine medical treatments and how inventions become the products that change how we work and play."

Sarewitz and Nelson say that when know-how is robust, it has a "go"—otherwise known as a course of reliable action. These "gos" help us implement solutions to societal problems like improving health care and reversing climate change. We can tout the knowledge we derive from science all we want, but without a "go"—or action—it won't have power because we can't use it to do good.

When it comes to the "knowledge is power" falsehood, you don't have to take my word for it, or the experts' for that matter. You can hear about it from thirty-three-year-old Connie Thompson. Connie grew up in a stable, two-parent home in an affluent area in southern California. Not wanting to leave the charmed environment of her childhood, Connie went to a top university near home. When she graduated, the pretty, intellectual twenty-two-year-old had her pick of jobs, including a coveted entry-level position at a boutique marketing firm on the east coast. Connie took the job, but quickly found herself unchallenged by the daily administrative duties. "I was definitely underutilized, and it was frustrating, because no one gave me a chance to prove my worth," she says. "The CEO, for example, saw me more as a personal servant than as a valuable staff member."

Connie was eventually given a few opportunities to create some campaigns for high-profile authors, which she did handily. Although she didn't have a lot of experience, Connie's natural creativity and intelligence allowed her to be better at the job than some senior-level staffers ten years older. However, because so much of her mental real estate was occupied by thinking about how she was still stuck at the entry level, Connie missed the chance to showcase her contributions and lost out on a promotion. Filled with negativity over the injustice of her situation, Connie decided to take some time off. This time of quiet reflection showed her that she couldn't simply sit around and wait for people to appreciate her. She had to take action to ensure that she was perceived in a positive light.

Connie returned to work, and little by little she began translating her knowledge and innate talent into visible activities that proved her worth to the organization. "Pretty soon everyone knew I was capable, and then I received the title, salary, and responsibilities that I craved," she says. "I stayed at the company for two and a half more years, and that period turned out to be a real blessing for my career. I just matured and grew so much personally and professionally."

Back to High School: The Popularity Factor

So knowledge and action equal power, and if people at work like you, that doesn't hurt either. There are scores of research studies on popularity in school, and most have indicated that popular children are viewed as better students and make and maintain friendships more easily. In 2009, however, organizational psychologists Timothy Judge and B. A. Scott at the University of Florida demonstrated that popularity plays a significant role in success in the workplace as well. They defined popularity as being "accepted by one's peers" and conceptualized it as a function of both an employee's personality and the situational position within his group. After studying two samples of employee populations, Judge and Scott reported that co-workers reliably agreed about who was popular on their team—and who wasn't. Co-workers also felt that an employee's popularity was associated with receiving more favorable treatment at work. Why? Judge and Scott suggest that popular employees are rewarding to interact with for both emotional and instrumental reasons. In addition to being "fun to be with," popular individuals are thought to increase co-worker status by association and make it easier to get things done.

Here are some painless tips for increasing your popularity on the office social circuit.

- **Be interested in other people.** Human beings love to talk about themselves and be listened to. By taking the time to learn about what a co-worker deems important and inquiring about those things, you'll make her happy and encourage her to like you. Example: "So your son plays basketball? How long has he been doing that?"

- **Shift attention away from yourself.** Don't chat on endlessly about what you and your girlfriend did over the weekend, and if a co-worker broaches a particular topic, don't immediately turn the discussion to your own experiences. Instead of trying to be admired, be admiring. Example: "Really, you grew up in Africa? It must be an amazing experience to have lived among so many different cultures."

- **Highlight other people's points.** Whenever you hear someone say something you like in a meeting, mention it and add your support. Example: "I think Joe makes a really good point. The holiday season would be a great time to pick up additional customers."

- **Eradicate self-consciousness.** People who lack confidence make others feel nervous and awkward. When conversing with co-workers, try to be natural and relaxed, without worrying about how you're being perceived. Example: "I left this shirt in the dryer way too long, huh? I guess I'll chalk this one up to a learning experience."

- **Organize team-building activities.** You don't have to be your department's cheerleader, but it's nice to occasionally take charge of getting the group together for drinks or another fun activity after work or during the holidays. Most people like to be social, and the individual who takes responsibility for being the organizer usually gets popularity points. Example: "The bar in the lobby is offering us two-dollar beers if we bring ten people in tonight. Who's in?"

■ **Help whenever you can.** Always be generous with your knowledge, expertise, and time without expecting anything in return. People like those they can count on in times of stress and who are willing to pitch in without making a big production out of it. Example: "I know that software program and could probably run the report in a few minutes. Want me to help so you can get out of here?"

Quantifying Your Contributions

Being good at your job isn't enough, and neither is working hard. You actually have to demonstrate results. Hard as it may be to believe, most junior and midlevel professionals haven't yet come around to this way of thinking. They still view their jobs as a series of completed tasks, and the idea of analyzing how well those tasks were achieved and what their efforts meant to the organization hasn't occurred to them. When I help my friends update their resumes or prepare for annual performance reviews, this notion of quantifying results usually comes up in the first five minutes of our conversation, because even those individuals with five to ten years of solid business experience will simply list their responsibilities without taking the additional step of letting the reader know how those responsibilities affected the bottom line.

Here's an example. A few months ago, I was talking to a twenty-seven-year-old operations manager named James in Pennsylvania. James was fortunate enough to be part of the innovations committee at his company, a Fortune 500 food manufacturer. A quarter of his job was to sit in a room and dream up new ways to make his company's products healthier, tastier, and easier to prepare, and devise new methods that would prompt consumers to purchase them in the store. What a cool job, right? James thought so too, and he had no problem communicating his enthusiasm on his resume with statements like:

- "Served on prestigious innovations committee that met at headquarters once a week."

- "Brainstormed and researched concepts for cutting-edge new products and extensions."

- "Held focus groups for consumers, store owners, and online retailers to assess the decision-making process leading up to purchase."

These statements sound interesting, sure, but they do leave some doubt in the mind of the reader as to whether or not the innovations committee (and by association, James) actually accomplished anything by spending one day a week holed up in a conference room. Was it simply a lot of talking, or did the company's performance improve as a result?

I encouraged James to go back to the committee and work with the other members to quantify their contributions. Most were very enthusiastic, as performance reviews were coming up in a month and they were all looking for ways to up their game. While the exercise did require some thought and analysis, James was surprised at how easy it was to get some of the data. Two weeks later James and I came up with the following resume statements:

- "Served as founding member of new innovations committee, which launched five new initiatives in half the time of the typical product development cycle."

- "Planned and executed rollout of in-store custom coupons, which increased retail purchases of canned fruit products by approximately $6 million."

- "Created an online advisory board for real-time consumer feedback on new campaigns, reducing marketing spending by approximately 25 percent in 2009."

Can you see how the reader's perception of James's role on the innovation committee might change from one resume version to the next? The latter example makes the work seem important, valuable, and critical to the food company's success. An employer reading this resume will feel much more confident that James can deliver results for her organization and that he's well worth his salary.

Note the use of the word "approximately." James obviously had to estimate some of these results, and there's no harm in that. However, he did have to be prepared to justify how he came up with those numbers. You should never put hard statistics in a resume or mention them in an interview unless you can back them up with an explanation, and for the love of God, please don't lie outright. A resume that resembles a two a.m. infomercial ("I earned a million dollars in two years without leaving my home!") will arouse suspicion and can end up doing more damage than a lackluster one.

Even if you're not on the market like James, you can protect your job and increase your chances of moving up by being able to communicate your quantifiable results at a moment's notice or when you're on the spot during your review. With this goal in mind, let's start with this exercise, inspired by Julie Rains at WiseBread.com:

WARM-UP

What were things like when you started your job and how have they improved since you've been there?

_____

_____

_____

_____

What did your boss say she wanted you to achieve when you first started? Did you meet these objectives? How has your performance been measured?

_____

_____

_____

_____

What notable accomplishments have you made despite adverse circumstances (e.g., company reorganization, industry slowdown)?

_____

_____

_____

_____

_____

ACTIONS

For instance, have you . . .

Opened new accounts?

_____

_____

Established new channels of distribution?

_____

_____

Created an infrastructure for any function(s)?

_____

_____

Eliminated unnecessary processes?

_____

_____

Developed new partnerships?

_____

_____

Reached new audiences?

_____

_____

Started a new division?

_____

_____

Automated a task?

_____

_____

Outsourced a task?

_____

_____

Expanded geographic territory?

_____

_____

RESULTS

And as a result of these actions, did you . . .

Increase sales?

_____

Reduce costs?

_____

Improve profits?

_____

Grow market share?

_____

Increase service levels?

_____

Achieve better quality or consistency?

_____

Reduce risk?

_____

Boost productivity?

_____

Lower employee turnover?

_____

Use these questions to nail down what you've achieved in your job to date, and as I mentioned before, don't be afraid to estimate. Also, even if a stellar level of performance is expected by your boss or your company, it doesn't mean that other employers won't consider it impressive, so my advice is to use anything that sounds compelling and can be measured.

Promoting Yourself Without Bragging

At the age of sixty-six, many Americans are ensconced in retirement, but not Marlene Caroselli of Pittsford, New York. In 1984 she founded the Center for Professional Development, an organization dedicated to helping working adults enhance their professional skills, and she's still going strong. Marlene spends her days consulting with clients like Lockheed Martin, Allied-Signal, the New York State Education Department, and the United States Office of Personnel Management, and she would never tell you that skill alone has gotten her ahead.

"The most talented are not always the most promoted, and sometimes we have to step out of our comfort zone to make sure the decision makers know what we're capable of," she says. Marlene was lucky in that she landed her first big contract with relatively little effort, and she knew that she had to use it to generate momentum. "Power does not flow to invisible people, and I knew I had to outshine my competitors. Once that first deal was inked, I subtly let other clients know that I was working with this large organization by weaving the big client's name into discussions," she says. "My visibility strategy was simple: win one important account and let accounts in secondary positions know that I had landed a star of the first magnitude."

Learning how to promote yourself and your accomplishments without sounding like you're bragging is no doubt an art, and to be honest, I'm still not wonderful at it. Most of the time, people say I'm too modest, but every now and then I'm sure I've completely turned my audience off. I've come to realize, though, that effective self-promotion is essential. Our work doesn't speak for itself. We have to speak for it. Basically, I think the secret is to relate your comments and actions to what others need, and to do so passionately. If you are enthusiastic when describing an achievement, then people will think that you're just excited and will be more likely to view you positively.

The first trick is to decide who really needs to hear about your work. You must identify the people (your boss, senior executives, etc.) whose respect and admiration you want to gain and then target your message to those people accordingly. The level of detail you provide to your boss will be different from what you give to the chief operating officer who you see in the elevator. Tailor your message to each individual, noting why each person would care about your accomplishments. What value have you brought to the company or department? How is your work making their jobs easier? Write down what you plan to say to each of these individuals in advance, and identify a time to talk to them when they aren't busy, stressed, or already conversing with someone else. Building genuine, long-term relationships will aid in your self-promotion efforts as well. Once you've established a point of contact, periodically remind these people what you're working on and show interest in refining your approach to meet their goals.

E-mail is another helpful tool for subtly spreading the word about your successful projects. Whenever you receive a message praising your work, you must ensure that your manager sees it. If she wasn't cc'd, forward the e-mail to her as an "FYI." If you're worried about coming across as a braggart, perhaps add a modest statement at the beginning, such as "Sue, I wanted you to see this and I know that I couldn't have done it without you and John." Similarly, if someone tells you verbally that he appreciated your work, ask him if he would mind e-mailing his feedback to your boss. He can also speak to your manager on your behalf, but if you have a choice, it's better to have the positive paper trail. Finally, my favorite use of e-mail in this context is to trumpet the outstanding results of a project with an e-mail to the whole department (or company, if it's a small one), thanking the team members who worked with you. This serves two purposes. It shows your collaborators that you appreciate their efforts, and it lets everyone else know that you did a stellar job managing the project.

Some of you probably try so hard to be team players that you push others into the spotlight rather than stand there yourself. If a colleague is generous or smart enough to give you credit when credit is due, thank her graciously and allow the focus to be on you for the time being. You've earned it.

Getting on the Executive Radar

In 1940 the Christian minister and civil rights champion Benjamin Mays became the president of Morehouse College, the first university for African American men in Atlanta. Shortly after his tenure there began, Mays met the fifteen-year-old Martin Luther King Jr., who had skipped both ninth and twelfth grade before enrolling as a freshman at Morehouse. King developed a close relationship with Mays and was an eager student, devouring Mays's ideas about the dignity of all human beings and the incompatibility of American social practices with American democratic ideals. Mays influenced King by his own example, guiding him toward the ministry and the preaching of a social gospel. Mays and King were so important in each other's lives that they eventually made a promise—he who outlived the other would deliver the eulogy at his friend's funeral. Sadly, on April 9, 1968, Mays saw King's mahogany coffin delivered to Morehouse on a wobbly farm wagon pulled by mules. "Martin Luther King faced the dogs, the police, jail, heavy criticism, and finally death; and he never carried a gun, not even a knife to defend himself. He had only his faith in a just God to rely on," Mays told the 150,000 mourners.

Benjamin Mays and Martin Luther King are just one of many famous mentor-protégé pairs—there's Socrates and Plato, Aristotle and Alexander the Great, Ezra Pound and T. S. Eliot, and Camille Pissarro and Paul Gauguin. Due in part to the prestige of their mentors, all of these protégés went on to be extremely successful themselves. It's a strategy that has worked time and time again: if you're truly terrific at your work and put yourself in a position to be noticed and admired by your boss and other senior level executives, you are much more likely to land on the fast track. Let's start with the boss. Even though you may think she's aware of everything you're contributing, this is most likely not the case, especially if you work in a large organization, with thousands of people, or a small organization, where every employee wears a variety of hats. If you want to be the person your manager considers her right hand, here are five musts:

- **Be willing and agreeable.** You know the moment in a team meeting when the boss apologetically asks everyone who can take on an undesirable task and all of your colleagues look down at the table? Be the one who looks her straight in the eye and accepts with enthusiasm. Once you take on the assignment, don't hold it over her head. Be gracious and complete it to the best of your ability. Take a leadership role in the group even if it's outside your comfort zone.

- **Sniff out new responsibilities.** If you're excellent at the job you're currently doing, then chances are you're ready for a new challenge. Look around your group and department and select a process or product that could be improved with your care and expertise. Make sure your boss knows how and where you're taking initiative, and don't neglect your day job in the process.

- **Manage your own time.** Managers hate when they have to keep hounding people to get their work done. Once a task is on your plate, your boss shouldn't have to mention it again. Complete assignments efficiently and on time, even if it means occasionally coming in early, staying online after hours, or neglecting your personal life.

- **Communicate actively.** Establish a relationship with your boss that goes beyond the pleasantries and your daily to-dos. Find out what his priorities are and the results he's expected to achieve on his end, and do what you can to further his causes. Learn the names of his wife and children and ask about them often. When his name comes up in conversation with others, speak in glowing terms. Schedule regular performance meetings so that your boss knows exactly where you'd like to take your career and so both of you are on the same page as to how you can get there.

- **Stay in the loop.** Your manager might not have time to keep up with all the goings-on in the industry and in your organization, so you should do it for her. Read the trade publications that have been sitting on her desk for weeks and provide her with a summary of interesting developments. If you hear or learn something critical about a competitor or another department, alert your boss immediately. Just be careful to err on the side of information versus gossip.

In addition to cultivating a strong relationship with your manager, it's also a good move to form solid friendships with other executives. As I mentioned in the previous section, alerting senior people to your stellar work and results is one way to foster these relationships. You should also attend company-sponsored events, sign up for volunteer or extracurricular activities, and organization-wide initiatives that will provide access to people you might not have the opportunity to interact with otherwise. When meeting an executive, maintain a clean and professional appearance, shake hands firmly, and offer him your business card. Even if you're nervous, watch that you don't talk his ear off. Instead, mention one or two points that show you've been keeping up with company developments and/or his career. Learn what he's working on and brainstorm ways you can contribute. Follow all in-person meetings with an e-mail the next day so that he remembers you.

Of course, executive blogs and social media sites like Facebook.com, LinkedIn.com, and Twitter.com are gold mines when it comes to establishing high-level connections inside and outside your organization. Follow the executives you want to get to know better closely online, provide them with useful links and industry updates, and comment on their posts. If you learn that an executive is attending or speaking at a third-party event, let her know that you'll see her there. I'll offer the usual caveat here, however—if you're going to use social media as a forum for engaging executives, make sure that everything on your profiles supports your image as a driven and engaged professional who's going places.

Becoming a Spokesperson

You can establish a strong public persona by becoming a trusted resource and the go-to person on a particular subject. The way to evolve into an expert is to always be learning. Even if you know more about your area than the average person, you're not done, for the world is always changing and there are new perspectives to explore. Make a habit of regularly consuming media and research directly or peripherally related to your field. Setting up a Google Alert and joining social bookmarking websites like Digg.com and StumbleUpon.com are time-efficient ways to get the latest and greatest information delivered to your desktop.

Suggests Doug White of Robert Half International (www.roberthalf.com), in his article for Yahoo! HotJobs, "From attending brownbag training workshops to getting involved with your company's mentoring program, take advantage of the professional development opportunities your employer offers. In addition, join industry associations, attend seminars, and seek relevant certifications."

Advertise your expertise by writing and submitting articles on your subject to internal or external publications or authoring a company-sponsored or independent blog. Volunteer to speak everywhere from local group meetings to international conferences, and share your knowledge and charisma with the world without leaving your desk by hosting online courses on sites such as Prfessor.com or discussing your subject on short videos you can post on YouTube.com or Viddler.com.

As you undertake these activities to become an expert, remember to look and act the part, and practice whatever skills are necessary to ensure your credibility. For example, if you strive to be your organization's social media expert, then your personal social media presence should be substantial, and if you want to be a media spokesperson, you should practice public speaking techniques and work with a public relations staffer to learn how to interact with reporters. In no time at all, you'll notice that your efforts are being noticed by more and more people.

BUILD YOUR ONLINE BRAND

Thanks to the proliferation of social media, your online reputation is just as important to your overall visibility as your in-office reputation. When a person searches for your name on Google, he should find information that showcases you as a reliable, enthusiastic, and loyal self-starter. When it comes to establishing an effective online brand, you should at least have the bare essentials—professional-looking Facebook and LinkedIn profiles and an online resume. By professional, I mean to err on the side of caution and not include any content that you wouldn't want splashed across the pages of the *Wall Street Journal*. I also recommend purchasing your name as a domain (e.g., Alexandra levit.com) from a service such as GoDaddy.com and developing an online portfolio of your work. Regardless of your industry, an attractively designed website that shows off your skills and experiences can go a long way toward convincing others of your worth and potential.

Your website should be as simple and easy to navigate as possible, with content that addresses the information needs of your target audiences (in-house executives, future employers, networking contacts, etc.). If you are an expert in multiple areas (e.g., green causes and architecture), think about whether it makes sense to illustrate them together or place them in different sections. Consider featuring case studies or examples of your work on the site, taking care to include details about your thought process and the concrete results I talked about earlier in the chapter. Manager, co-worker, or client testimonials are an excellent addition to a personal website. "Third-party affirmations show that you are truly capable of doing what you say you are, and they also reveal a person's personality and go beyond what can be said on paper," says Heather Huhman, founder of Come Recommended (http://comerecommended.com), a helpful website for soliciting testimonials. "Recommendations are often the make or break aspect in a hiring decision."

If you want to include a blog as part of your site, survey your industry first to see what blogs currently exist and where there is a need for more thought-provoking and helpful content. Once you've decided on a niche, gain traction by commenting on and linking to other blogs in your space and by making sure your blog is listed on your company's intranet (and the company's external website if appropriate). It may also make sense to offer a monthly or quarterly e-newsletter on your site and place an e-mail sign-up form on the home page. This will serve two purposes: it will remind your contacts periodically of your expertise and it will allow you to build a robust e-mail database for networking purposes.

Finally, make sure your contact information is housed in a prominent location, and that your site shows up first when people search for your name in Google. You may even wish to take this a step further and incorporate certain keywords into your site so that it comes up when people search for your area of expertise. Include a link to your site in your e-mail signature and in all online profiles so that it becomes a natural extension of every communication.

MYTHBUSTER'S SUMMARY

- You can be the most talented employee your company has ever hired, but if your contributions aren't visible and people don't value what you do, it simply won't matter.

- Knowledge does not in fact equal power. Today, there is no shortage of knowledge to be gleaned. It's not what you know, but the specific action you take as a result, that determines your success.

- Popular people are more visible because others want to be around them. Increase your own popularity by shifting attention away from yourself and showing interest in your co-workers.

- You can protect your job and increase your chances of moving up by being able to communicate your quantifiable results and subtly promote them to your boss and senior executives.

- Establish a strong public persona by becoming the go-to person on a particular subject. Be a perpetual learner and showcase your knowledge by serving as an organization spokesperson and creating a convincing online brand.

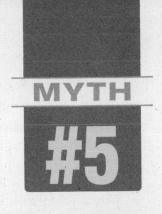

MYTH

#5

It's Best to Climb the Ladder as Fast as Possible

n August 2005, Hurricane Katrina struck the Gulf coast of the United States and became one of the five most deadly natural disasters in the country's history. The most severe effects were felt in New Orleans, which flooded due to a failure of the levee system. With millions of families stranded, scarce food and drinking water, and grave safety concerns, New Orleans turned to the federal government—specifically the Federal Emergency Management Agency (FEMA).

This was a disappointing decision. From the beginning, FEMA acted as if it had never handled a relief operation before. Funds were misplaced, partner organizations were uncoordinated, and everything took more time than the desperate people of New Orleans had. The media blamed Michael Brown, the

Bush-appointed head of FEMA, to such an extent that the U.S. Congress formally investigated the matter.

Michael Brown is a prime example of why it's not always best to get promoted as quickly as possible. Before President Bush tapped him for the FEMA position, Michael was the commissioner of judges for the International Arabian Horse Association. He was widely considered to be good at this job, but he simply did not have the right experience for a career in emergency preparedness. Nevertheless, he took the FEMA job, which was higher paying and more prestigious—and got in way over his head. In reality, Michael Brown likely wasn't and isn't a bad guy, but he was so vilified in the public eye that he had no choice but to resign, reportedly with the question: "Can I quit now?"

According to Josh Clark, a writer for HowStuffWorks.com, Michael Brown's situation is not uncommon in public and private sector organizations. A person who excels at his position is often rewarded with a higher position and eventually reaches a level that exceeds his field of expertise. This is called the Peter Principle, a concept that was put forth in the 1960s by Laurence J. Peter, a psychologist and professor of education.

"In a hierarchically structured administration, people tend to be promoted up to their level of incompetence," Peter explained. "The cream rises until it sours." Why does this happen? Well, you probably know that companies prefer to hire from within because internal candidates are considered to be more trustworthy and have a better understanding of how their organization works. For the same reason, qualified internal candidates keep getting promoted until they aren't qualified anymore, and at that point they will be stuck in a situation where they feel insecure about their abilities and produce work of less value to their companies. "In fact, most often those at the top of the organizational chart are the farthest removed from any particular issue and least capable of making good decisions and solving complex problems," says Ed Poole, an organizational consultant and the author of *Lessons from Empowering Leaders*.

Sometimes these leaders get fired and sometimes they're left alone, but one thing is for sure: people who have been promoted too soon get pretty stressed trying to fake it 'til they make it. Susan Barry of Panama City, Florida, is one such leader. After just a few years in the restaurant and hospitality business, Susan was promoted to an executive-level position as director of sales and marketing in an upscale hotel. She was just twenty-five years old. "I think I got that job because I had made it clear to anyone who would listen that I wanted to be the boss. My predecessor had really struggled in her position and was ultimately asked to resign, so it was easy for the corporate folks to pick me because I had a proven track record and I was absolutely chomping at the bit to do the job," she says. "They also knew that they could get me really cheaply because I was relatively inexperienced."

Susan dug into her new position, working at least twelve hours every day. "I felt like I had to know everything, and I was doing whatever it took to make sure I didn't look stupid," she says. "I was so focused on making sure no one figured out I was too young for the job." Her efforts paid off. Susan was promoted several more times and was selected to open two new hotels. She eventually landed in Atlanta, where she butted heads with some old-school, Southern male owners.

"I had to work three times as hard as someone older just to

prove that I could do my job," she remembers. "Those owners made my life a living hell by questioning my every move." Though she had decades left in her career, Susan was burned out. She walked away from the hospitality industry.

The potential to become a victim of the Peter Principle is greater than ever today; after all, the pending mass exodus of baby boomer employees means that millions of twenty- and thirty-somethings are getting promoted into leadership positions at younger ages. And the Peter Principle is a very good reason why the myth that it's better to climb the ladder as fast as possible doesn't hold up. But if Peter hasn't convinced you, I'm about to talk about some other promotion realities, including the fact that money and a stellar career don't buy happiness, the fact that some people are better doers than leaders, and the fact that job burnout is common when your higher titles come with longer hours and heavier responsibilities.

This chapter will also address how to make the most of your time at the entry or mid level, and in the event that you're a rising star who fears she can't stop the train, I'll close with a discussion of when you should—and should not—accept a promotion, and how to turn one down gracefully if it isn't the best thing for you.

Money and Promotions Don't Buy Happiness

Many junior level and midlevel employees want to get promoted as quickly as possible because they believe that an increase in income will lead to greater life satisfaction. Harvard University psychologist Daniel Gilbert begs to differ. In his book *Stumbling on Happiness*, he concludes that money increases happiness only when it lifts people out of abject poverty and into the middle class. Once you're in the middle class, however, and your basic needs are taken care of, income increases aren't likely to affect your happiness one way or the other.

This idea has been supported by global surveys that ask people how satisfied they are with their lives on a scale from 1 to 7 (1 being "not at all satisfied with my life" and 7 being "completely satisfied with my life"). Among American multimillionaires, the average happiness score is 5.8. Want to know who else had a score of 5.8? People of the cattle-herding Masai tribe in Kenya, which has no electricity or running water. And even people who have just barely escaped from homelessness and starvation—slum dwellers in India—rate themselves at 4.6.

Growing countries are slightly less happy than countries with slower growth rates, according to Carol Graham of the Brookings Institution and Eduardo Lora, as reported in a 2010 article by David Brooks in the *New York Times*. The United States is much richer than it was fifty years ago, but this has produced no measurable increase in overall happiness. Brooks also writes that people aren't happiest during the years when they are winning the most promotions. Instead, people are happy in their twenties, dip in middle age, and then, on average, hit peak happiness just after retirement at age sixty-five.

If you want to be happier, don't focus on getting promoted—focus on improving your relationships. Brooks says that the daily activities most associated with happiness are sex, socializing after work, and having dinner with others. According to one recent study, joining a group that meets once a month produces the same happiness gain as doubling your income. According to another, being married produces a psychic gain equivalent to more than $100,000 a year.

Stellar careers are notoriously rough on romantic relationships. Consider the so-called Oscar curse, in which nine Best Actress winners in the last twelve years have split with their partners shortly after their acceptance speeches. In 2010 alone, 2009 winner Kate Winslet separated from her director husband, Sam Mendes, and 2010 winner Sandra Bullock broke up with reality star husband, Jesse James. Inside and outside Hollywood, some speculate that men are intimidated by successful spouses and their egos can't sustain a wife's meteoric rise. This is not to say that women should deliberately hold themselves back professionally, but if a relationship is of priority, then it must come before the career. The research doesn't lie. Those who are able to sustain gratifying marriages will be happier with their lives despite career setbacks, whereas those without life partners they can rely on will be more dissatisfied with life no matter how many promotions they get.

Don't Underestimate the Power of the Doer

In every company I've worked in, there have been too many chiefs and not enough Indians. In other words, everyone wants to be running the project but few people actually want to do the work. That's why I loved Nancy Lublin's article "Do Something: Let's Hear It for the Little Guys" in the April 2010 issue of *Fast Company*.

Lublin writes that the business world has overdone the whole leadership thing and that we're not spending enough time crediting the folks who turn all the visionary stuff into tangible reality. The world needs more people who can follow intelligently, ask questions, and crunch numbers to make sure the boss's grand plan actually works.

When an organization has too many chiefs, operations are redundant, groups are inefficient, and plans never get off the ground. And if you're a chief in an organization like this, it doesn't matter what your title is—you won't be successful because you won't be able to get results. On the other hand, if you do a standout job at the mid level, you'll feel good about your performance and will probably have your pick of employment opportunities. The simple reality is that it's often easier to accomplish more and make more of an impact as a doer than a leader.

Some people are so good at "doing" that getting promoted leads them in a direction they don't want to go. John Burnham, for example, spent his childhood in Denver and joined the U.S. Navy at the age of nineteen. "I managed to score quite well on the GCT—the military version of an IQ test—so I was offered specialized training in electronics," he recalls. John was hired by Ampex, a supplier of high-capacity digital storage systems, as an electronics technician. In just a few years, he was promoted three times—to line foreman, to test engineer, and then to general foreman, a position in which he managed sixty people.

How did he pull this off? "I always tried to develop the competencies of my subordinates so that my operation could run without me, and therefore I was available when juicy assignments came along," he says.

As the accolades piled up and John's prestige increased, he began to develop a sense of entitlement. "People deferred to me and I felt like I deserved it," he says. But one day, John was called to task at corporate headquarters in Redwood City, California, because his facility had been accused of accepting and using faulty parts. "Management ruled in our favor, but the problem was, we were guilty. I destroyed the career of our accuser, when he was right and we were wrong. I knew I should feel bad, but I didn't, and that scared me."

Disliking the person he'd become, John left Ampex in his early thirties and pursued careers in aviation and petroleum. "In every job since Ampex, I've had the opportunity to take on management responsibilities, but the fear of having to make another ethical sacrifice keeps me from accepting."

Worrying about ethical compromises isn't the only reason many doers don't want their boss's job. Sometimes they don't want to give up the work that they love in order to manage others doing that work. "I equate getting promoted to being a baseball player who is suddenly told he now gets to be the manager of the team," Carlos Portocarrero writes on his Writer's Coin blog. "I play baseball in a city league in Chicago and I've been playing since I was seven years old. I love playing baseball, but managing all the players and their expectations, playing time, and so on, is a totally different ball game."

Pace Yourself or Risk Crashing and Burning

Fifty-six-year-old Doug Paddock was born in Chicago and raised in the picturesque Ozark Mountains of Arkansas. His parents built two cattle operations, and Doug's dream was to spend his life working on the ranch. However, the properties were sold and Doug went on to get a degree in accounting from Arkansas Tech University and launch a career with Price Waterhouse in Little Rock. "I was unhappy with accounting work, so I decided to go to seminary," he says. "After graduating in 1980, I spent the next ten years serving in a variety of ministerial roles."

Doug eventually went to work with one of his parishioners in the insurance business, and he was quite nervous at first. "The position was straight commission and I was afraid of starving," he says. "I don't know if it was fear, skill, or the fact that I was a good con man, but pretty quickly I was making more money than I'd ever earned in my life. By the end of my first year in the business, I was number two in the nation for bringing in new clients, and I'd received the 'President's Club' ranking." Doug continued his ascent in a variety of geographic locations, and the constant change led him to ignore the symptoms of depression and burnout. He began drinking heavily, and by 2004 he found himself unable to do his job. "I made history in the company by being the only one to resign from such a high role. I was making a tremendous living, and then one day I couldn't do it anymore," he laments.

Does Doug's story sound at all familiar? Let's look at a quiz to determine if you might be in a similar situation. Please circle *T* (True) or *F* (False) for each of the statements below:

You don't sleep well at night and find it difficult to summon the energy to get out of bed in the morning.	T	F
You have trouble focusing on any one task when you're at work.	T	F
Your social life consists only of work-related events.	T	F
You find yourself snapping at co-workers and clients.	T	F
You find it hard to feel a sense of accomplishment for a job well done.	T	F
You don't take vacations, and if you do, you bring your work with you.	T	F
You get defensive when friends or family members say you work too much.	T	F
You're experiencing more aches and pains than usual.	T	F
You've been eating or drinking more than usual.	T	F

If you found one or more "True" statements, consider this: people who climb the ladder at a quick pace are at risk of collapsing under the weight of their longer hours and extra responsibilities. Job burnout can have serious mental health consequences, including depression, anxiety, and alcohol and substance abuse.

Your answers above should provide you with important clues as to whether burnout is becoming or has already become an issue for you. You might proceed by talking to your boss about how you can make your current job more manageable. Perhaps an additional hire could ease your load or a senior team member can be tapped to mentor you on the aspects of your role that are foreign to you. I'd also recommend taking advantage of your organization's employee assistance program (EAP), if available. Such programs provide counseling and resources to help employees cope with burnout. Asking for help may be a hard pill for high achievers to swallow, but admitting you can't solve a problem on your own is actually the hallmark of a rational and mature individual.

In the event that you're coasting along and simply enjoying your success, you should pace yourself. Remember that a career is a marathon, not a sprint, and make a conscious effort to keep burnout from creeping in. Here are some ideas to that effect:

- Get back to basics. People who experience a dizzying rise often lose sight of what made them select that career in the first place and their job's place in their overall life scheme. Spend a morning writing down where you'd like to see your life in five years, and describe how you plan to use your current job to get there. Having a better handle on your personal big picture will make it easier to combat burnout.

- Do something for yourself once a day. Instead of spending all of your waking hours trying to be all things to all people, set aside a half hour to do something that has no other purpose but to make you happy. It could be as simple as sitting in the park on the way to work.

- Preschedule time with friends. If you wait until you have a free moment to call a friend to invite her to dinner or a movie, you may never see her again. Instead, build social engagements into your weekly calendar, setting aside time each week to spend with the people who mean the most to you.

- Support those who are less fortunate. Volunteering is a terrific way to refresh your outlook and give back to the community that has supported your success. Not sure where to begin? Check with your organization's social responsibility and human resources departments to determine if there are interesting activities already in place for employees.

- Employ generous deadlines. Instead of packing every day full of meetings and tasks, be realistic about how long things actually take and leave plenty of cushion room to cope with last-minute assignments and unforeseen delays. Develop long-range calendars for complex projects so that you can sustain your productivity over time and avoid running out of steam halfway through.

- Get out of your office. I'm sure you've heard that exercise improves mood because it releases chemicals called endorphins. No matter how much work you have to do, resist the urge to hole up. Get up from your chair and stretch. Go to the gym or take a walk around the building. When you sit back down again, you'll feel rejuvenated.

Use Entry- and Mid-Level Time Wisely

SEEK OUT TRANSFERABLE SKILLS

Stuart Smith's background is as corporate as they get. After earning a degree in accounting from the University of Cincinnati, Stuart went to work for IBM and was promoted to manager at the age of twenty-six. "This was insanely young by IBM standards," he says. "When the company downsized in 1989, I left with a six-figure severance package." He had not even turned thirty.

After a brief stint at Price Waterhouse, Stuart was lured to Dell by a few other ex-IBM employees. Things there moved quickly. Stuart started as a corporate cost accounting manager and was quickly promoted to controller, worldwide operations, and then director of corporate finance and planning. "I got to spend a lot of time with Michael Dell and other senior executives," he recalls. "I was viewed as a problem solver, and when I was promoted again—this time to vice president of materials and logistics—I thought I was ready to move out of finance."

In his new role, Stuart was responsible for the supply chain and distribution for Dell's Americas operations. He had little experience in this area, but the company had the perception of him as an up-and-comer who could do anything. "I devoted my life to Dell and was generally regarded as the smartest guy in the room. I had Michael's ear. My team wanted me to succeed," he says.

But Stuart was in over his head. His first assignment was to fire a few problem executives, a task that didn't go particularly well. "Leading a large, complex organization draws upon a much different set of skills than I had," he says. "In particular, I hadn't had time to develop my communication skills. I didn't do a good job of clearly articulating a strategy that my organization could own and execute. Team building and fostering consensus were my weak points and stunted any further growth as an executive."

When it came time to reorganize the company again, Dell's leadership decided it needed a more mature executive in Stuart's position. Stuart was offered a midlevel management job in his original department, corporate finance, which he declined. "My pride simply wouldn't allow me to backtrack," he says.

Stuart's story is a profound illustration of why it's often better to take your time at the junior and mid levels and build transferable skills that will add value in any executive job and aren't likely to become obsolete. If you rise without mastering critical competencies like communication, people relations, project management, sales, marketing, and finance, you may be setting yourself up for failure.

When your daily responsibilities are keeping you on your toes, it can be difficult to build skills that are not directly related to your current job. It's important to put a plan in place that will allow you to focus on transferable skills in the long term. The first step in this process is to make a list of desired skills based on the attributes of the most successful senior leaders in your field. For example, after being mentored by a vice president who is known for effectively managing client meetings, you may decide that you need to hone the skill of client relations. Next, it's time to get specific: you should write down your goals and motivations and the activities associated with acquiring the skill. It might look something like this:

Transferable Skill: Client Relations
Goal: Manage a client meeting in its entirety.

What I'm going to do: Talk with my boss about my desire to manage Client X's next meeting solo. Then schedule the meeting, complete the agenda, run the event, and take charge of follow-up.

Why I want to do it: I'm looking toward being promoted to vice president next year, and managing client accounts without supervision is a critical competency of that role.

When I'm going to do it: Client X's next meeting is scheduled for June—two months from now.

How I'll measure my success: After the event has been completed, I will collect feedback from the clients and from my colleagues who attended.

What transferable skills do you want to hone in order to be successful at the next level? Take a blank sheet of paper and complete the above bullets for one or two desired skills.

Even after you've gotten some solid experience in each transferable skill you target, always look for ways to take it up a notch. Staying marketable, particularly at the mid level, means that your development never stops. You should jump at the chance to do any internal training courses, job rotations, committee roles, or temporary assignments that will bolster your transferable skills.

People who are happy in their jobs may neglect their resumes for years, but this is a mistake because it usually means they are also complacent in keeping track of all the progress they've made in various positions. If you're planning to stay with your organization for the foreseeable future, that's great, but make sure you keep an up-to-date roster of all the projects you've worked on and the results you've achieved and create a running portfolio of work samples where appropriate.

Assessing Whether Promotion Is Right for You

LEARN WHAT YOU DON'T KNOW

When I talked to Ed Poole about young professionals who rise too quickly, he warned me of the danger of being "unconsciously incompetent," meaning you don't know what you don't know. You can avoid this outcome by putting yourself in a position to objectively evaluate your strengths and weaknesses. "Observe your own work patterns and behaviors and do the same for your colleagues in parallel positions," Ed suggests. "Take a look at how leaders in higher-level positions go about their daily work, how they set goals, how they interact with subordinates and superiors, and how they help other people grow in the organization." Consider asking managers, colleagues, and direct reports (possibly via a 360-degree review process) for direct or anonymous feedback regarding how you can improve your leadership skills—before you are in a sink-or-swim situation. Securing a mentor and taking advantage of professional development activities can also be helpful in this respect.

ASK THE RIGHT QUESTIONS

Before he was an organizational consultant, Ed Poole spent decades as a public school administrator wandering from job to job. "The new jobs I took were always promotions. I moved from middle school principal to high school assistant principal and principal to associate superintendent, and finally superintendent of schools," he says. "I made my decisions based on external validation and what others thought I should be doing."

The superintendent job became difficult when Ed's leadership style wasn't readily accepted by his subordinates, and in the late 1990s, he landed in a psychiatric care unit with clinical depression. "The greatest gift of that experience was the realization that, stripped of my fancy job titles, I had no idea who Ed Poole was," he says. "And as I recovered, I realized that I should have asked myself some questions before blindly accepting the superintendent job. For example: Is the position a good fit for me? Will I enjoy being a superintendent? How does this position fit into my long-term career plans? What kind of support can I expect? Will I be allowed the opportunity to make mistakes and learn from them so they won't be repeated?"

Ed brings up an important point. Tempting as it may be, just because you are offered a promotion doesn't necessarily mean you have to accept it. In fact, Laurence Peter suggested that self-aware employees consider the extra responsibilities that come with a promotion and turn down the job if they feel the job exceeds their capabilities, an action he referred to as "Peter's Parry." If you are a rising star who senses that you've been offered a promotion you may not be ready for, here are some issues to think through:

- **Can you handle the workload?** How are others at this level getting along? Are they drowning or are they able to maintain some semblance of work/life balance?

- **Do you want the workload?** What are the daily responsibilities of individuals at this level? Do their days involve activities you enjoy, like traveling, attending strategic meetings, and managing finances?

- **Will you be adequately compensated?** Will the increase in your salary be worth the extra hours and responsibilities?

- **Does this promotion take you in the right direction?** Will this promotion allow you to clearly map your path over the next five years? Will you be able to continue your climb, and is the final destination somewhere you want to be?

- **Are you prepared to manage the staff?** What do you know about the people you are inheriting? Do you already have positive relationships with some individuals? Is there a collaborative spirit among the group?

What if you've carefully considered these questions and you feel that accepting the promotion is not the right move to make?

Ed Poole thinks that it's possible to turn it down without losing your job. "If you and your boss have a positive working relationship that is built on openness, honesty, and trust, then the conversation should not be difficult and your point of view will be understood and appreciated," he says. Best practices for saying no to a promotion include:

- **Give it a few days.** Even if you think you know your answer right away, nothing can be gained from jumping the gun. Tell your boss you'd like to have two days to consider the offer and you will come across as mature and thoughtful rather than brash and ungrateful.

- **Be gracious.** Speaking of which, when you return to your manager to report your decision, start by thanking him for the opportunity and telling him how much you appreciate his faith in you (for example, you might say: "I'm really flattered that you feel I've made such strides, and I'm looking forward to making X, Y, and Z contributions in this role next year"). Be careful not to act as if his decision was a bad one (for example, don't say: "I just don't think I'm the right person for the job").

- **Sell them on the status quo.** Tell your manager why you feel it's best for the organization if you stay in your current position. You might say, for example, that you really love your job and still feel like you could add a lot of value to the role. You might also talk about uncompleted projects that you want to personally see to fruition.

- **Be flexible.** Remember that by turning down the promotion, you are creating a problem for your boss—now he has to fill that job some other way. So as best you can, try to compromise and perhaps even come up with an alternative solution. For instance, maybe you can volunteer to assist in hiring a more senior individual and take on more responsibility until that person can get up and running.

Turning down a promotion is a difficult rite of passage in a rising star's trajectory, but it's better for your long-term career to exceed expectations in your current position and move up when you're ready than be forced to wear shoes you can't possibly fill.

MYTHBUSTER'S SUMMARY

- Rising stars must be careful not to fall victim to the Peter Principle, in which a person who excels at his position is rewarded with a higher position that exceeds his field of expertise and leads to incompetence.

- Promotions don't buy happiness. Once you're in the middle class and your basic needs are taken care of, income increases aren't likely to affect your happiness one way or the other.

- It's often easier to accomplish more as a doer than a leader. If you're a leader in an organization with too many chiefs, you may be unable to generate results due to a lack of consensus. However, if you do a standout job at the mid level, you'll feel good about your performance and will probably have your pick of opportunities.

- People who climb the ladder at a quick pace risk collapsing under the weight of longer hours and extra responsibilities. Job burnout can have serious mental health consequences, including depression, anxiety, and alcohol and substance abuse.

- Take charge of your own career by deciding whether a promotion is right for you and turning it down strategically if you're not ready. Meanwhile, make the most of your time at the mid level by seeking out transferable skills and collecting feedback on areas for improvement.

#6

You'll Get More Money Because You Earned It

I n the summer of 2008, the board of the United Way of Central Carolinas made an unprecedented announcement. Chairman Graham Denton apologized to his community for the compensation package given to the organization's president, Gloria Pace King. "We made a serious mistake, and the continued success of our United Way is threatened by an erosion of public confidence and trust resulting from the current controversy," he said in a statement.

Earlier that year, residents had gotten wind that Gloria earned over $1.2 million, and they were irate over what they dubbed an inflated salary for the head of a local, nonprofit organization. Although Gloria had been the most effective president in the group's history—a critical part of raising a record $45 million in a single year—and she boasted tenure of fourteen years, the board let her go.

If anyone had earned a raise, it was Gloria. She put the rest of her life on hold to take the United Way of Central Carolinas to places it had never gone before, and she was widely considered to be one of the most successful leaders in the entire United Way network. Sure, she made a lot of money, but hardly an outrageous amount when compared to other CEOs. But public perception is a powerful thing, and not only was Gloria denied a raise, she was fired.

Gloria isn't the only one who didn't get the compensation she earned. These days, it seems that only the baby boomers remember what it was like to do an impressive job at work and receive an impressive raise to match. The rest of us have been making do with 1 to 3 percent standard of living increases, or worse, no increases at all. Ken Abosch, head of North America compensation for Hewitt Associates (www.hewitt.com), a global HR consulting firm, tells us that the rate of growth in salary increase budgets at most U.S. employers has been decreasing steadily for the last twenty to thirty years, with the greatest declines occurring in the last ten years. "Given the magnitude of labor cost and the increasing competition from a global economy that includes workers in other countries who do similar work for significantly lower wages, the days of 4 percent salary increases are quickly becoming a thing of the past," he says.

Nevertheless, we all grew up with the myth that we will be financially compensated for stellar performance. And it's so easy to look at your garden-variety A-list celebrity and the guy sitting in the cubicle next to you and think, "I work harder than him, so

I should be earning the big bucks." Unfortunately, the effort you put into your job often does not correlate to a pay increase—even if you've gotten results. This chapter will explore how compensation actually works from a business perspective, what your manager is thinking when deciding how to dole out raises, and why some people are paid more than their counterparts regardless of performance. I'll also share strategies for asking for a raise so that, despite the obstacles, you are one step closer to getting the compensation you deserve.

The Business of Compensation

In his ten-year career as a strategic planning consultant, thirty-three-year-old Shawn Phillips, of Pittsburgh, had reliably gotten a raise every review period. During his 2010 performance review, Shawn's manager told him that their main client had sent in a glowing recommendation for Shawn and was extending the firm's engagement for another year. So Shawn was understandably shocked when his manager then said that Shawn would be receiving a 10 percent reduction in pay due to a "market adjustment." Apparently the firm hadn't recovered from the effects of the recent recession and most clients were paying considerably lower fees. The company couldn't afford to keep going unless it cut everyone's pay, including that of the top performers. "It was a rude awakening when I realized that I could be a star but wouldn't necessarily be compensated for it," Shawn says.

The first thing you must understand about the business of compensation is that compensation is a business. One of the most important factors that affects employee compensation is the overall financial performance and health of the company. "At the beginning of each fiscal year, companies set operational and strategic goals, and if those benchmarks and objectives aren't reached, employee compensation will be impacted," says John Robak, chief operating officer at Greeley and Hansen (www.greeley-hansen .com), a water engineering and management firm. "If a company reaches its targets, then it determines exactly how much employees will receive from the amount that was budgeted for salary increases, but if performance is not strong, an organization may institute a companywide salary freeze in order to protect its long-term future."

Even in good economic times, some companies are limited in their ability to provide salary increases for deserving employees. For example, "many start-ups usually have little cash and have to reward employees with stock to conserve it, and companies governed by unions can usually only reward increases that are specified in the contract," says Hank Federal, a senior consultant in the compensation and rewards practice of Findley Davies (www .findleydavies.com), an HR consulting firm.

Some organizations that aren't start-ups or unionized are simply guilty of playing fast and loose with their profits. "Many companies choose to believe that high periods will last longer than they actually do, and the associated extravagant spending eventually results in the company failing to meet its targets and undertaking salary reductions," adds Mika Liss, currently a board adviser and formerly an executive vice president at Tescom (www .tescom-intl.com), a global professional services firm.

Fixed internal policies and/or salary structures may also affect an organization's ability to raise salaries freely. For example, an organization (especially if it's in the public sector) may have pay grades, or fixed salary ranges, that prevent managers from increasing compensation beyond the amount predetermined by an individual's level, title, or length of service. "There is a market value for every job, and so salary is designed to reflect competitive pay for each job," says Vasu Mirmira, senior director of compensation and organizational development for CNO Financial Group (www.cnoinc.com), an insurance conglomerate. "Salary range maximums are a cost containment mechanism intended to keep the company from overpaying for a particular skill." Additionally, compensation may be centralized with a few, higher-level executives, and it may only be addressed with employees at certain times of the year.

Other factors affecting a company's compensation are what competitors are giving their employees and market costs. "Organizations are focused on attracting and retaining the talent needed to run the business, and having a close eye on the compensation of competitors ensures that an organization is not providing too much or too little to employees," says Abosch. "And market factors such as cost of labor, cost of living, and the demand for goods and services weigh heavily on employee compensation."

Abosch says that market conditions associated with the economic downturn of the late 2000s led 20 percent of U.S. corporations to reduce employee salaries. He also notes an uptick in situations like Gloria's. "We are seeing an increase in governance and external scrutiny," he says. "Organizations need to ensure that their compensation programs are reasonable and defensible."

A Manager's Thought Process

Even if your organization is in good financial health and market conditions are favorable, your salary increase still depends on the person doling out the raise money. It's not uncommon for this person to be a higher-level executive in your group with whom you don't typically interact. You may be a stronger performer than a colleague but not as visible, and this could negatively affect your compensation. Let's assume for the sake of argument, though, that your boss has the power to decide who gets a raise and who doesn't. What's her thought process?

According to Federal, the first consideration is how to keep all staff members happy. "No supervisor relishes the conversation in which she does not give an individual an increase. She wants to be liked and giving a zero increase will not make her popular." The desire to be liked is one reason some managers take the path of least resistance and spread the raise budget across all employees equally, regardless of performance. "This approach creates less conflict and minimizes the amount of effort a manager has to invest in the decision-making process," adds Abosch. "It's more typical of a manager who has not internalized the pay-for-performance concept and does not have accountability for doing so."

All the executives I consulted mentioned that managers want to be able to justify compensation decisions, and this usually means that they reward the best performers. But not always. "A manager might decide that an employee needs to be motivated to improve his performance, and so he will give an increase to that person," says Robak. And Liss shares an example in which a manager had second thoughts about an employee's great performance. "This salesperson did really well, but didn't get a raise because his manager felt that (a) his commissions should already reward him for his increase in sales and (b) his sales cost the company more than they were worth due to excessively lengthy sales cycles."

Similarly, some individuals may have a high performance rating, but a talent management rating that indicates they are well placed at their current salary level. Mirmira explains: "Talent management is a forward-looking view of your potential, and a high performance rating does not automatically translate into a high talent management rating. It is very possible for an employee to be a consistently high performer, but, in the eyes of the manager, have limited potential for taking on larger assignments." With some high performers, there's also the issue of consistency. "A manager may overlook a person whose performance spikes every so often—since a spike implies downward movement as well—in favor of a person who stays at a reliably above-average level," says Mirmira.

Of course, in considering a manager's thought process, let's not overlook the simple but relevant question of whether she likes an employee or not. "Office politics and whether an employee is well-liked play an important role in compensation decisions," says Richard Block, a partner and employment law expert at the firm Mintz, Levin, Cohn, Ferris, Glovsky and Popeo (www.mintz.com). Where do you think the word "kinship" comes from? Human beings have been rewarding the individuals closest to them for millennia, and your boss is no different.

Twenty-nine-year-old Ana Ramirez currently works for a

for-profit educational institution in the southern United States. Ana, who is friendly and charismatic, admits that she's not the hardest-working employee in her organization. But she's the most visible and the best liked, so she got a raise when her colleagues did not.

As the executive assistant to the CEO, Ana sees her company's leader every day. She has gotten to know him on a personal level, and the two of them are close. "The fact is, I didn't have to demonstrate and document my accomplishments as diligently as my colleagues did. The CEO has a lot of flexibility in how he compensates high performers, and I was someone he wanted to reward," Ana says.

If you are not one of your manager's favorites, or worse, if you and your boss have a difficult relationship, you may find that outstanding work is not enough to secure an increase. And you'd be surprised how easily he's able to justify his decision.

Why Equal Employees Are Not Paid the Same

Sheila O'Malley grew up in Chicago as a self-described "girl next door." At the University of Illinois she majored in accounting, and following graduation she worked at a series of controller jobs at Fortune 500 companies in the Midwest. "Every time I took a new position, I got a salary increase, so after a while I was doing pretty well," she says.

In her late thirties Sheila decided to try her hand at consulting, and she found that it suited her well because she enjoyed the diversity of the work. On one project, she was placed on a team with three other senior accountants, all of whom were male. "We had the same background, education, and position, and had just received similar reviews from our client," Sheila says. "One day we got to talking about our rates, and I learned that I was making 20 percent less than everyone else."

Sheila approached her manager about the disparity, hinting that there was sexual discrimination occurring. "Women are relatively new to the accounting world, and there is a perception that management shouldn't invest in people who are just going to have babies and leave. I don't think my situation is unusual— it's still an old boys' club," she says. Although Sheila's boss did not formally acknowledge the pay gap, he did give her a substantial increase at her next review.

In a 2010 article for *Harvard Business Review*, "Investigating the Pay Gap," Sarah Green says that the median salary of a woman is still only 78 percent of a man's. This means that women have to work sixteen months to earn what men make in a year.

According to the American Association of University Women, the gap between men's and women's salaries starts immediately after entering the workforce. Just one year out of school, a woman earns 80 percent of what a man earns. After controlling for industry, type of job, prior experience, and other characteristics, women's earnings are 95 percent of men's. The unexplained 5 percent gap is viewed as evidence of bias. After ten years, despite controlling for the factors above, the average woman earns only 88 percent of what the average man earns and the unexplained gap has widened from 5 percent to 12 percent.

Also as Green reports in her article, the Center for American Progress went a step further and tracked wage gaps by age and occupation. The organization found that by the end of their careers, male managers have made $635,000 more than their female peers. Apparently, wage discrimination doesn't get better as you get older, more seasoned, or better educated—it gets worse. If you're female, no matter how well you perform, your raise simply might not be as high as your male colleague's.

Besides gender, human resources experts tell us that there are a variety of reasons you could be making less money than a same-level colleague who was hired at a different time under different circumstances. "It's a common practice for organizations to hire new employees at pay levels that vary from the pay levels being provided to existing employees," says Abosch. "New employees who have been recruited to leave other jobs will often not make that move at the same level of pay because there is a certain 'risk premium' associated with a new situation." Even someone who makes a lateral move is likely to receive at least 10 percent more money at his new organization.

Your colleague might also make more money because her market was stronger than your market. "Another factor that influences salary level is the supply and demand conditions in the labor market at the time of an employee's hiring," says Abosch. Robak agrees. "Current economic and labor conditions play a role. At a particular time, there may be a high demand and significant competition for experienced candidates, and those individuals will be paid more."

Of course, as Abosch notes, the most defensible rationale for paying same-level employees different salaries is that each employee comes with different knowledge, skill sets, and aptitudes. "Even if two employees are hired for the same job, one individual's qualifications could more positively impact the speed of work, innovation and originality, quality of thought, and results," he says.

Defensible or not, this means that if your colleague is better than you in some respect (e.g., she has an MBA and you don't, or she did a certain kind of internship and you didn't), you may be destined to make less money for all of your days at that company, regardless of your performance. You may start out lower, and even if you're doing the same job with similar results, it is entirely possible that you will never catch up.

Requesting a Salary Increase

Often, whether you get a raise or not is not in your control. But the good news is, sometimes it is and it never hurts to ask for one. Take twenty-five-year-old Genevieve Masaccio for example. Genevieve was your classic overachiever—serving as class president, getting A's, and playing sports at her high school in Portland, Maine, and graduating with honors from Smith College.

Shortly after finishing school, Genevieve took a job as a receptionist in a publishing house in Boston. Just a few months later, she was bumped up to a nonadministrative position, but did not receive a salary increase. "I got the typical 3 percent increase at my annual review, but that didn't account for all of my increased responsibilities," she says.

Over time, Genevieve felt her wallet being stretched. "When I thought about how much value I was adding to the company and how little I was being paid, I started to feel resentful." So she visited the website www.salary.com and researched the salaries of midlevel publishing professionals in Massachusetts. Her suspicions that she was underpaid were confirmed, and Genevieve decided to approach her manager. "I printed out the Salary.com data and jotted down some talking points."

Though she had a great relationship with her boss and deliberately chose a time for the discussion that wasn't too crazy, Genevieve was nervous about broaching the topic of money. "I just wasn't comfortable with it," she admits. "I grew up thinking that good things came to people based on the quality of the work they did. I had no idea that I'd have to advocate for myself."

But advocate she did, saying to her boss, "There's something I want to talk with you about. I've been thinking about my salary and the work my job requires. I did some research, and I'm wondering if we can chat about what I'm making." She emphasized how much she loved her job and enjoyed working for the company. To Genevieve's surprise, her manager agreed that she was earning too little and agreed to approach the chief operating officer about increasing Genevieve's salary outside the traditional review cycle.

When people ask me if they should approach their managers about a raise, the first thing I tell them is to think carefully about whether or not they've earned it and how receptive their boss will be. This means sitting down in a quiet place and measuring your performance against the goals you set with your boss (see chapter 1 for more on goal setting). Ask yourself if you've contributed to the bottom line and exceeded expectations to such an extent that your company should pay more money to employ you.

It helps to have external proof as well. "If you're doing a great job, it should be evident to everyone around you," says Mika Liss. "Your manager should know it and hear it from the people around you. Praise from peers is more valuable than self-promotion."

Have you received positive feedback from people other than your boss in the form of e-mails or company awards? Is your manager aware of this feedback? Think this through for a few moments and jot down your thoughts here.

_____

_____

_____

_____

As I've said throughout the chapter, context is critical. If you make your request without considering your boss's state of mind (for example, cornering your boss when she's under a tight deadline), you will fail. Rather, pick a time—like Friday after lunch—when she seems as relaxed and unstressed as possible. Also before proceeding, make sure you understand all of the business factors at play (your organization's financial status, preexisting compensation policies, etc.), because these could affect your boss's ability to help you. You'll save yourself and your manager a lot of pain and discomfort if you are aware of the limitations ahead of time.

I also recommend Genevieve's approach of researching your own market value. Check out compensation surveys by the U.S. Department of Labor (www.bls.gov/ncs) and Hewitt Associates (www.hewitt.com) and salary websites such as www.salary.com and www.payscale.com to determine how your compensation compares to what other same-level employees in your geographic area are earning. Talk to people at third-party professional associations in your field, and ask industry colleagues how much their organizations would pay someone at your level. If your organization offers perks such as bonuses, stock options, retirement contributions, tuition reimbursement, memberships, or retail discounts, be sure to take those into account.

There's also no substitute for instinct. You know your company's culture better than anyone, so even if you've rationally evaluated your request according to the parameters above, go with your gut as to whether asking for a raise will be perceived well. If you honestly feel you have a good shot, then go for it, because, as Genevieve learned, advocating for yourself is essential. If you don't ask, you don't get.

The best time to ask for a raise is just after a stellar performance review because your boss will be anticipating it. If you have just been promoted or received new responsibilities that are typically associated with a higher-level position, it is appropriate to broach the subject of a salary increase.

If you can, try for an informal setting like over coffee. Before the meeting takes place, role-play it with a loved one so that you can practice a tone that sounds friendly and assertive rather than bitter and entitled. Once you sit down with your manager, start positively. You might, for example, say something like: "I've gotten so much out of working here and really appreciate your mentorship and the opportunities you've given me."

Then ask if she'll consider a salary increase in light of your recent performance. You might lead off with: "Now that I've been doing the work of a senior account manager for almost a year, can we consider an increase in compensation to reflect these new responsibilities?" As clearly and concisely as possible, go over the highlights with some concrete examples. Focus on the benefits your boss and the company receive from your contributions rather than the additional money you need or desire. For example, you should say something like: "Because I can do the job of both an account manager and a programmer, I'm saving the company an additional salary" rather than: "I need to be making more income to pay for my wedding next year." And don't bring co-workers into the discussion by saying: "Well, Gary Bishop has only been working here a few months and I know he's making way more than me." "Speak to your value to the organization rather than speculation or rumors about what other employees are earning," recommends Robak.

If you don't get the answer you want, don't act angry or disappointed or say something to the effect of: "This is completely unfair" or "I can't believe what I'm hearing." Calmly ask your manager what you need to do to receive a raise and if it's possible to revisit the issue in the near future. Perhaps say something along the lines of: "Okay, I understand where you're coming from. Am I correct that if I take on three additional accounts before the end of the fiscal year, you will be able to consider a compensation increase then?"

No matter how frustrated you feel, do not say anything resembling, "Well, now I'll have to consider whether I'll be able to stay here" or "I guess I'm not as valued here as I thought I was." Refrain from giving any ultimatums unless you are prepared to resign that day. Even once it becomes clear that you won't get an increase, listen carefully to what your boss has to say and keep an open mind. In lieu of cash, she may be able to offer you concessions such as extra vacation time or game seats in the company box. She may also agree that you deserve a raise, but say that she doesn't have the authority to give you one. If this is the situation, ask her if the two of you can schedule a meeting with the executive responsible for your compensation. Don't go to the executive without your boss's knowledge. Note that if a meeting with a higher-ranking executive isn't an option for logistical reasons, ask your supervisor if she can pursue the issue on your behalf in four to six months.

Sometimes, a more passive boss will try to "yes" you out the door with no intention of following through. This is why you should take careful notes on everything that is discussed and any verbal promises she makes and recap them in an e-mail you send her immediately after the discussion.

MYTHBUSTER'S SUMMARY

- The first thing to understand about the business of compensation is that compensation is a business. One of the most important factors that determines employee compensation is the overall financial performance and health of the company.

- Fixed internal policies (such as pay grades) and market considerations (such as what competitors are paying their employees) also affect an organization's ability to raise salaries freely.

- When deciding who should get a raise and who should not, managers consider how to keep all team members happy, how they can reward the employees they like, and how they can justify their decision.

- Same-level employees may not be paid equally because of gender or because they were hired at different times under different circumstances.

- If you are going to ask your boss for a raise, think carefully about whether you've earned it, and then evaluate your request in the context of current conditions inside and outside the company.

The Problem Isn't You, It's the Organization

Manny Ramirez is widely considered to be one of the best baseball players of the last decade. He has career totals of 527 home runs and 1,725 RBIs, while hitting for a .314 average over sixteen years. All these totals put him near the top of every category. A native of Santo Domingo in the Dominican Republic, Manny has played for a succession of prestigious major league baseball teams, from the Cleveland Indians to the Boston Red Sox to the Los Angeles Dodgers. He never stays with one team for long.

Writes Matt Steinbach in a 2009 article, "Manny Ramirez Needs to Stop Being Manny": "Everywhere Manny Ramirez goes, controversy follows. He has always been ridiculed for his behavior around the media and his strong and quirky personality. Ramirez is never afraid to say what's on his mind or do whatever he feels like. There will be games where he doesn't feel like playing, so he doesn't show up. He constantly requests trades because it seems as if he is never happy. Because of his personality, many teams don't want him."

Despite his considerable talent, jumping from position to position hasn't worked out particularly well for Manny Ramirez, and this wouldn't surprise Mark Suster. Mark is a serial entrepreneur who joined GRP Partners to focus on early-stage technology companies after selling his second company to Salesforce.com. He is enormously respected in the entrepreneurial and venture capital communities, which is why the April 2010 post on his blog, Both Sides of the Table, caused quite the stir. Here's what Mark had to say:

"I never hire job hoppers. Never. They make terrible employees. Even in a focused search through recruiters, I'm always looking to eliminate the job hopper. If I'm sent a stack of 10 resumes, the first thing I look for is how long the person has been at their past four or five jobs. If they've had five jobs of two years or less each—buh bye. Why do they make such bad employees? Job hoppers are the first people to the door. They're self-centered. They don't have a sense of loyalty to you despite the risks you took with them. They don't understand the word commitment. As a startup founder, you will have dark days, and you will only have a handful of people you trust. That person you're thinking about hiring who's 30 and had a bunch of jobs isn't one of them about right now."

He continues: "I've been accused of not trying to get to know the person but just judging them by their past. Um, yes. Of course! It's like a woman who is dating a man who has had six wives and cheated on all of them before divorcing them but she somehow thinks SHE will be different. Philanderers establish patterns that they don't easily break. Career job hoppers are no different."

Job hoppers believe in the classic myth "It's not me, it's them." You might secretly buy into it too—maybe you haven't yet learned that you take yourself with you wherever you go, and that jumping from job to job is no use because you're likely to run into the same situations over and over. And in a climate like this, it's also a good way to give yourself a heart attack, because every time you make a switch, you have to contend with a new set of complexities in a company just trying to survive.

Why is this myth so pervasive? Organizational psychologist Keely Killpack has some insights. "It's hard for human beings to accept that their own character flaws are making them unhappy," she says. "Our own self-destructive behaviors are harder to pick out than the same behaviors in others."

And even if you do realize you have a problem or two, you might not want to do anything about it. "Fundamentally, people are reluctant to change," says Killpack. "Working on ourselves requires effort and intention, and it involves our ego. For many people, it seems easier in the short term to blame it on the company and go someplace else."

"Short term" is a key phrase here; job jumping because you consistently find yourself in negative situations will not benefit your career in the long term. Not only do you have to start over each time, but explaining to hiring managers why things didn't work out at your previous company can be a very tricky proposition. "We get irritated when someone complains about being a victim, and the more that person vocalizes his feelings, the more skeptical we become," says Killpack. "We begin to think that the blame should be placed on the individual's personal shortcomings, not his places of employment."

Killpack points out that people who can't or won't take responsibility for the role they play in difficult workplace encounters rarely achieve high levels of success. "Most people at the top will confidently tell you about their failures, mistakes, and challenges along the way," she says. "On the other hand, people who blame their lack of progress on others are often deliberately held back because they are perceived as unfit for leadership."

It's time to ditch the fruitless exercise of repeating the same scenarios and expecting different results. Instead of searching in vain for the perfect work situation, why not take a look at yourself and determine how you can change things from the inside out? Your job satisfaction is more in your control than you may think, and in this chapter I'll discuss how to adjust your attitude by changing your thinking, increasing your tolerance for frustration, and learning self-awareness. Then, in case you need some additional help or follow-up, I'll conclude with advice about pursuing coaching or therapy.

The Power of Attitude

Forty-nine-year-old Jake grew up with a father who worked at a string of paper mills in the southern states, living everywhere from Alexandria, Louisiana, to New Johnsonville, Tennessee, a town without a single traffic light. He made an impact on his high school class by cracking constant jokes and dressing in rainbow suspenders with buttons like the alien Mork from the popular 1970s sitcom *Mork and Mindy*.

Jake unconsciously dreamed of being an actor, but, lacking a specific plan, he allowed himself to be pressured into college. "I had obtained my amateur radio license in high school, so I thought that electrical engineering might make sense," he remembers. "I wound up going to Nashville State Technical Institute, a two-year school, where I enrolled in the computer technology program." However, Jake disliked his course work intensely and began skipping classes. Not knowing how much longer he'd be able to stay in school, he got a job as a cook at Pizza Hut.

Unhappy with the direction of his life, Jake began complaining at work. "The manager would ask me to do something and I'd mumble wisecracks under my breath," he admits. "If a lot of orders came in, I'd whine about having too much work. No matter the topic, I'd find something to gripe about." Then, one day during a busy rush, Jake aired his grievances in front of his manager and found that his boss had lost his patience. "He led me back to the storage area and laid down the law. He said I had a bad attitude and that if I wanted to keep my job I'd better change it now."

Jake was embarrassed and ashamed. "He was right, and by bringing it to my attention, he allowed me to improve." Jake didn't take any extreme actions—he just stopped complaining. "I started saying positive things, like complimenting a co-worker. And I asked to become a waiter so that I could invent a new persona." He also finally decided to acknowledge his dream of becoming a working actor. In the process of moving to Nashville to take acting classes and transferring to a Pizza Hut there, Jake says he became one of the best waiters the restaurant had ever had.

His enthusiasm for his work was infectious. "Customers requested me and I consistently received more tips than others," he says. "Once, I spilled an entire glass of soda on a customer, and even that guy couldn't stay angry with me. I stayed positive and did everything I could to fix the situation, and the customer realized that. He even tipped me."

In the end, Jake didn't pursue acting professionally, but he doesn't regret any of the efforts he undertook, because they helped shape the positive person he became. Currently an HR manager for a financial services firm, Jake always looks for candidates who have a great attitude above all else. "Despite less experience and fewer skills, a person who is positive will win every time."

Whether you work at Pizza Hut or GE, it's easy to see how the work world's unfair realities can anger people. After all, policies don't always make sense, managers don't always understand us, and the environment is often out of our control. Developing a bad attitude is a natural consequence when we believe that someone or something is keeping us from succeeding or doing our best work. However, it's important to realize that in the end, negativity only makes you look bad, and it's a career killer because other people will avoid working with you no matter how smart and talented you are.

Staying positive when it feels like the universe is conspiring against you isn't easy, and a part of you may even think it's impossible. Except it isn't. I'll never forget learning in a college psychology class that we can choose our response to individual situations by focusing our thoughts instead of allowing them to run amuck.

I'm a glass-half-empty person, so when I encounter an unpleasant situation that disrupts my day, the first thoughts that pop into my head relate to the worst-case scenario. For instance, if someone stands me up for an interview at a conference, the first thing I think is that the person has blown me off because he is inconsiderate of my time and doesn't think my work is important; the second is that my editor will be angry with me because I'll miss my deadline. What I've learned to do, though, is move on from this initial negative reaction by first letting go of assumptions and then analyzing whether the situation is objectively as bad as it seems.

Jumping to conclusions is a natural reaction in a situation like getting stood up at a conference without an explanation. It's very tempting for me in such a case to assume that I should take the brush-off personally. But thinking this way doesn't make me feel better, and it may not even be accurate. Who's to say that the person didn't get stranded by the hotel shuttle? What if he lost his iPhone and consequently his calendar? Maybe he got sick or caught up in another meeting. It's quite possible that the situation has nothing to do with my article or me, and I have to adjust my thinking accordingly.

Sometimes I have to argue with myself, and I do this in the form of a piece of paper that I divide into five columns. In the first column, I write exactly what occurred (e.g., the conference interviewee stood me up). In the second, I describe the negative thoughts that instantly appeared (e.g., he doesn't think my piece is important). In the third, I write out evidence that supports the negative thought (e.g., the conference interviewee didn't call me to reschedule), and in the fourth, evidence that disproves it (e.g., he agreed to the interview in the first place even though his conference schedule was booked solid; the press liaison told me that typically 50 percent of interviews scheduled during this conference don't happen due to uncontrollable factors). In most cases, I'll see that the evidence disproving the automatic negative thoughts far outweighs the evidence supporting it, and I'll have no rational choice but to give some credence to alternative explanations that don't hurt quite so much. I write out these alternative explanations (e.g., transportation snafu; lost calendar) in the fifth column.

I might also turn the paper over and write out the worst-case scenario for not getting this particular interview (e.g., I'd miss my deadline and my editor would be angry with me). Then I'll jot down all the things I can do to keep this worst case from becoming a reality (e.g., try to connect with the conference interviewee on the phone; find another interviewee with a similar background). Generating these additional solutions helps me see that the worst-case scenario is not inevitable or likely, and I'm able to change my thinking and attitude about the situation as a whole.

Now it's your turn to analyze a recent negative event. Take a blank sheet of paper and divide it into five columns. Label the columns as follows:

- Situation

- Automatic Negative Thoughts

- Evidence to Support Negative Thoughts

- Evidence to Disprove Negative Thoughts

- Alternative Thoughts or Explanations

On the back side of the paper, write down what will happen if one of your negative thoughts comes to fruition. How will you handle it?

If you are someone who's accustomed to dwelling on negative thoughts, this exercise will probably feel ridiculous at first, like some pop psychology b.s. that might work for naïve people but not for you. And this sentiment won't go away overnight. Sometimes I'll be writing out alternative thoughts and explanations and I'll still say to myself, "I don't buy it." Just remember that discomfort is a good thing because it means change is under way.

It's unreasonable to expect that you'll be able to transform every difficult situation into a fortuitous one with a few strokes of the pen. But if you get into the habit of paying attention to and challenging how you perceive the events in the work world, you'll find that in general you can do away with negative thoughts and get past the hurdles of professional life much more quickly, and you can ultimately improve your attitude.

Combating Unrealistic Expectations

One of the biggest culprits of a bad attitude is unrealistic expectations about the world, because having a belief that something should or must happen in order for you to be content sets you up for frustration and disappointment. Here are some examples of poisonous *should* or *must* statements you might be tempted to make during your work day:

- My company *should* have a policy against this.

- This project *must* be funded.

- My boss *should* be more empathetic.

- The VP *must* understand this approach.

The implication of such statements is that if events aren't logical and people don't behave in the way you think is right, you will crumble to pieces. Using the word "should" or the word "must" in a sentence usually means you are holding on to an irrational expectation, and having irrational expectations can be detrimental to your well-being and to your career. Once your colleagues see you flipping out trying to correct a situation that is beyond your control, they will respect you less.

But how do you keep the *shoulds* and the *musts* from overtaking your life? Start by asking yourself if your life will really be ruined if things don't go exactly the way you hope. Instead of insisting that something *should* happen, rephrase it as something you *would like* to happen and plan how you are going to cope if it doesn't happen. You're still being cognizant of your own point of view, but removing the expectation will keep you from reacting emotionally.

Let's suppose you were just transferred to another department and you are angry about it. Here is how you might rephrase irrational expectations that come up:

Irrational expectation: They should have transferred someone else.

Healthy response: I would like them to transfer someone else, but they have their reasons for transferring me instead. I can't change this situation, so how can I use this new position to propel my career forward?

Irrational expectation: Work shouldn't be this traumatic.

Healthy response: I would like it if work wasn't traumatic, and if I think about it, an internal transfer isn't the most traumatic thing that could have happened to me. I could have been laid off, or worse, I could live in a war zone.

Irrational expectation: Management must change its mind.

Healthy response: I would like for management to change its mind, but I do not have control over other people's actions. Furthermore, if management does not change its mind, I won't die. I will go on living and it's my choice whether I do it in a negative or positive frame of mind.

Dale Furtwengler's tendency to create inflexible judgments and rules about the people and events in his workplace caused him to change jobs every few years for a period of two decades. As an accountant, Dale had a knack of creating efficient systems, but he always fell into the trap of thinking that his colleagues should react to his efforts in a certain way. When they didn't, Dale would grow bored and frustrated, and he'd end up moving on. He endured much hardship before he realized that many of the conflicts he encountered in his various jobs were self-created because he had overly aggressive goals and unrealistic expectations. In his current role as a consultant, Dale (www.pricingforprofitbook.com) comes into work every day with an open mind and the patience to understand perspectives that are different from his own.

Managing Frustration

When I asked organizational psychologist Keely Killpack why people develop bad attitudes that eventually cause them to jump ship, frustration was the main reason she cited. Killpack noted—and decoded—some common business world frustrations:

> "I can't believe I put up with this place."
> *Translation:* "Having to play along with office politics is unjust. I wish I could just say what I feel."

> "I can't believe I've worked here ten years and I still can't make things happen."
> *Translation:* "I haven't reaped the benefits of my dedication or the success I desire."

> "I can't believe he's getting all the credit for my project."
> *Translation:* "I'm the one who put the effort into this initiative and the organization isn't acknowledging it."

Another key ingredient for frustration, says Killpack, is the lack of control that a person perceives for the outcome of their work. In psychology, this is called locus of control, a concept that was originally developed by Julian Rotter in the mid-twentieth century. One has an internal locus of control if he believes that he controls his own destiny, and he has an external locus of control if he believes that his destiny is controlled by other forces like authority figures, fate, or God. Over the last half century, psychological research has determined that males tend to be more internal than females, older people are more internal than younger people, and people at higher levels in the organization are more internal than junior-level staffers.

In general, having an internal locus of control is viewed as more desirable, since these individuals tend to be more achievement oriented. They are more persistent and work longer and harder to get what they need or want. It's better from a mental health perspective too, because when you feel that you can affect the outcome of your work, you are more satisfied and have a greater sense of accomplishment.

If you are a person who is prone to an external locus of control, this could be a major cause of your agita at work. Fortunately, there are things you can do to develop an internal locus of control. For example, you can:

- **Acknowledge your own choices.** Just being alive means that you make thousands of small choices every day, and those small choices add up to make a major impact on your life. As for the bigger choices, usually you do have the power to take control of the ones that are really important.

- **Set achievable goals every day.** I talked about long-range goal setting in chapter 1 already, but I bring this up again here because being able to check even minor things off a list each afternoon will improve your self-esteem and increase your internal locus of control.

- **Practice making decisions.** Work on the skill of listing and evaluating the pros and cons of each option and coming to a conclusion on your own rather than relying on the opinions of others.

Of course, as I talked about earlier in the chapter, changing your thinking can also go a long way when it comes to your perception of control. If a thought such as "I'm helpless and there's nothing I can do" finds its way into your head, quickly dispose of it by focusing on what you *can* do to better the situation.

Some people also have low frustration tolerance, meaning that they are irritated by life's minor inconveniences. For instance, if FedEx is late delivering your package, you might yell at the customer service rep or stare blankly at your computer while your anger simmers just below the surface. Since these types of situations crop up all the time, it's in your best interest to rein in your negative reaction to them. The first step here is to imagine how things could be worse. As an example, FedEx could have lost your package instead of delivering it late, or you might lack the funds to buy the contents of the package in the first place or pay for their shipping. You may also want to try a little of what psychologists call "exposure." This involves making a list of the everyday situations that annoy you (driving on the highway at rush hour, waiting on hold for a customer service representative, etc.) and subjecting yourself to them gradually so that you can increase your tolerance. As you're experiencing these situations, you might ask yourself why you're frustrated in the first place. Is it that you feel helpless or put out? If so, you might put processes in place to eliminate that negative feeling. For example, I get frustrated by sitting in meetings because they make me feel inefficient. I find that if I schedule these to last just thirty minutes (enough time for quick status updates and to-dos), I'm not nearly as anxious about my time being wasted.

My husband, who's a psychologist, recommends an additional strategy to increase your ability to cope with frustration, and that is to put the frustrating situation in context. You can say, for instance, "Of all the upsetting things that have happened to me in my life, getting chastised by my boss in front of my client was a 7 on a scale of 1 to 10, but not getting a seat on the subway this morning only gets a 2."

Negativity Quick Fixes

If you've taken steps to change your thinking, combat unrealistic expectations, and manage frustration and you're still experiencing more negativity than you'd like, you might try these tips:

- **Hold your judgment.** Unpleasant emotions often result from the fact that we are too hard on ourselves and others.

The reality is that human beings are going to make mistakes and won't always act consistently. Instead of expecting perfection and evaluating yourself or the people in your life as all good or all bad, try to be more accepting. Remember to judge the behavior rather than the person. If a colleague does something you don't like, you can call her on it, but it's up to her whether she's going to change.

- **Focus on the present.** Once upon a time, I expended a great deal of energy worrying about what happened in the past and what was going to happen in the future. You will feel more serene and in control of your life if you focus on what you are able to accomplish in the present moment.

- **Let mistakes go.** High-achieving individuals tend to beat themselves up when they don't handle a situation well. Since you don't have the power to turn back time, learn from the experience, make fixes if you can, and allow yourself to move on.

- **Have Thanksgiving today.** No, I'm not talking about the turkey and sweet potatoes—although those sound good too. Make a list of all the things in your life for which you feel lucky or grateful (a stable job, a nice place to live, a traffic-free commute, etc.). Like the column exercise I described earlier in the chapter, this one might be the reality check you need to release some of your negativity.

Knowing Yourself

Thirty-six-year-old Nichole Bazemore grew up as an army brat. She was born in Hawaii and lived in Colorado, North Carolina, and Germany before she graduated from high school. Surrounded by siblings, Nichole enjoyed introspective time in her room writing poems and nurturing her imagination. When it came time for college in Ithaca, New York, Nichole chose to study television and radio. "I was attracted to the idea that a reporter's workday is never the same, and the fact that TV news was a prestigious career choice," she says.

In Nichole's first job out of school, she was a "production grunt" for CNN in Atlanta. "I was resentful. I felt that I was too smart to rip scripts and fetch coffee. My attitude drove me to isolate myself from co-workers and burn bridges," she says. She left CNN to take a reporting job at the ABC affiliate in Waco, Texas. Although Nichole was sharp, poised, and well-spoken, she noticed that the plum reporting assignments and the weekend anchoring gig were given to another reporter who was not articulate or very bright. "She and the news director were Caucasian, whereas I am African American, and so I assumed that she was given the better jobs because of her race. Again, I found myself having a 'me versus them' attitude."

Nichole kept jumping jobs. She held a few more in television and then did stints as a flight attendant, direct sales associate, career counselor, and writer. "In nearly every position, there came a point where I butted heads," she says. "The word used most frequently in my performance reviews was 'defensive.' I always perceived that I was being mistreated on the job and that my negative experiences were the fault of those I worked with, so I kept moving."

After eighteen years and several repeat experiences, Nichole decided to take a closer look at the role she played in her employment situations. "I realized that I'm not the easiest person to deal with. I've had a chip on my shoulder, a sense of entitlement, and I'm overly sensitive and a control freak," she says. She made an effort to change her behavior and learned how to identify and present her skills and talents in a way that conveys value. And when things don't go her way, she doesn't take it personally. Today, as the owner of consulting firm Simply Stated Solutions (www .simplystatedsolutions.com), Nichole has a much better sense of who she is and what she does—and does not—do well. She's always working on herself and, as a result, is better able to maintain healthy and authentic relationships with her clients.

Self-awareness, which may be defined as being conscious of what you're good at while acknowledging what you still need to learn, is one of the most underrated leadership skills. Apparently, it's also one of the rarest. According to Chris Musselwhite's article for Inc.com and the Change Style Indicator, a research study on management styles that has been conducted for two decades, leaders are often unaware of how their behavior affects others. Also, in appearing as if they know everything all of the time and disguising their mistakes and weaknesses, they diminish their credibility with colleagues and reports.

If you're a job jumper like Nichole, a lack of self-awareness may be what's holding you back. In organizational psychology research, self-awareness is often incorporated under the broader umbrella of emotional intelligence, or EQ. Let's look about how this discipline came about and how you can use it to your advantage.

The Rise of EQ

Born in 1946, Daniel Goleman was the baby boomer child of two college professors in the liberal arts. Growing up in California, Daniel found it difficult to adjust to life at Amherst College in straightlaced New England and transferred to the University of California at Berkeley. An anthropology major, Daniel was heavily influenced by several gifted professors, including the sociologist Erving Goffman. Nevertheless, he returned to Amherst for his senior year, writing an honors paper on mental health in historical, anthropological, and social perspectives and graduating magna cum laude.

Daniel received a scholarship to Harvard from the Ford Foundation and enrolled in the clinical psychology program. His mentor was David C. McClelland, who had developed a well-known theory about the drive to achieve and was researching the competencies that distinguished star performers from average ones. Daniel grew interested in the ancient systems of psychology and the meditation practices of Asian religions and spent time, predoctorate and postdoctorate, in India and Sri Lanka. After writing his first book, *The Meditative Mind*, he took a job at the magazine *Psychology Today*.

It wasn't until his twelve-year tenure covering psychology for the *New York Times*, however, that Daniel hit upon the concept of emotional intelligence, or the ability to identify, assess, and manage the emotions of oneself, of other people, and of groups. Although Daniel didn't coin the term, his bestseller *Emotional Intelligence: Why It Can Matter More than IQ* was responsible for "EQ" entering popular culture.

Daniel watched with wonder when EQ showed up in cartoon strips like *Zippy the Pinhead* and in *New Yorker* illustrations. He saw boxes of toys that claimed to boost a child's EQ, lovelorn personal ads trumpeting it in those seeking prospective mates, and hotel room shampoo bottles with EQ quotes printed on them. Emotional intelligence could be expressed in languages as diverse as German, Portuguese, Korean, and Malay and by religious scholars in all faiths.

Daniel continues to advocate for EQ from his home in the Berkshire Mountains, cochairing the Consortium for Research on Emotional Intelligence in Organizations based in the Graduate School of Applied and Professional Psychology at Rutgers University.

Sure, emotional intelligence is everywhere, but what exactly does it entail? Here are brief descriptions of EQ components:

- **Emotional Awareness:** You understand the emotions you're feeling and how those emotions affect your behavior and performance.

- **Accurate Self-Assessment:** You are aware of your own strengths and weaknesses, you're open to feedback, and you learn from experience.

- **Self-Confidence:** You present yourself with poise and are not afraid to voice unpopular viewpoints.

- **Self-Control:** You don't act on impulse but instead remain composed and focused under pressure.

- **Innovation and Adaptability:** You uncover fresh ideas to problems. You are flexible and handle change well.

- **Achievement Drive:** You constantly seek ways to improve results and hold yourself accountable for strong performance. You persist in your goal despite setbacks.

- **Commitment and Initiative:** You understand the organization's core purpose and will make sacrifices in service of that. You are able to mobilize others and go above and beyond what's expected of you.

- **Understanding and Developing Others:** You listen well and show sensitivity to others' points of view. You reward people's strengths and encourage their improvement through specific feedback and strong mentoring.

- **Team Building:** You create like-minded groups, model team qualities like respect and helpfulness, and share credit.

- **Political Awareness:** You are aware of important formal and informal relationships, who's friends with whom, and how things actually get done in the organization.

- **Influence:** You are skilled at gaining consensus and drumming up support for your projects. You challenge the status quo and enlist others to help implement relevant changes.

- **Communication:** You are able to read between the lines when conversing with others, you speak in a straightforward manner, and you seek mutual understanding.

- **Collaboration and Cooperation:** You share information and resources and balance your focus on a task with attention to relationships.

- **Conflict Management:** You address problematic situations proactively, bringing them to light with tact and diplomacy. You encourage open discussion and help to orchestrate mutually beneficial solutions.

It may sound like there is a lot involved in being emotionally intelligent, but truthfully, a lot of these components go together, meaning that if you're strong in one, you'll naturally be strong in the others. For instance, people who are strong in self-confidence are often equally adept in inducing change, gaining cooperation, building teams, and resolving conflicts. Therefore, in addition to honing each component, you can employ several strategies that will help you improve your overall EQ in the workplace:

- Identify the situations that cause you to lose your cool. Think about the things that routinely stress you out or make you upset and flustered—like being criticized by a client for something that isn't your fault—and rehearse reacting in a civil manner the next time these situations come up.

- Pay attention to the physical signs of negative emotion. As I mentioned in the previous chapter, be on guard for the warning signals that you're losing control. As soon as you observe them, politely excuse yourself so that you can calm down before proceeding with the conversation.

- Monitor nonverbal cues. Emotionally intelligent people are cognizant of not just what they say, but also how they're saying it. In the midst of a conversation, make sure that you're using appropriate eye contact and facial expressions. Position yourself next to the person you're speaking to, but don't get so close that you invade her space. Your tone should accurately convey your message. Smile, unless you're in the process of telling the person something she doesn't want to hear. You should also ensure that you accurately read others' nonverbal cues so that if you're not getting a good response to your message, you can quickly change your approach.

Seeking Coaching or Therapy

Behind most successful leaders is a strong coach or mentor. Henry VIII, for instance, was just seventeen years old in 1509 when his father died and left him the throne of England. An able-bodied boy, Henry excelled in hunting, jousting, and gambling. He was a risk taker by nature, and so his father's conservative approach to rule was not for him. Although Henry VII left his son two primary counselors, Henry VIII soon appointed advisers who shared his point of view, including Thomas Wolsey, a Catholic cardinal.

For nearly half of Henry VIII's reign, the wily and driven

Cardinal Wolsey served as lord chancellor and for all intents and purposes controlled domestic and foreign policy for the inexperienced king. He negotiated truces with France and the Holy Roman Empire and centralized the national government. He also encouraged Henry in the king's divorce from Catherine of Aragon, thus setting the stage for England's permanent break from the Catholic Church. Cardinal Wolsey is in large part responsible for Henry VIII being known as one of the most famous monarchs in European history.

From humankind's earliest days, mentors and coaches have been a significant ingredient in the careers of many accomplished individuals. Nearly five hundred years after Cardinal Wolsey guided Henry VIII, forty-six-year-old Lisa Rosendahl was desperately in need of someone to help her make the transition from the military to the business world. "I was working as an HR manager for a small, privately owned manufacturing company, and it was me against the system," she remembers. "I was always very capable, but when we got down to brass tacks I was defensive and self-protective." The president of the company selected a leadership coach to work with Lisa and her team, and at first Lisa was thrilled.

"At first, I listened to what she said and used it as information to help me work in the face of others' deficiencies," she says. "I didn't realize that I was part of the problem, and my relationship with the owner broke down. I ended up leaving the company." Lisa moved to a higher-level HR manager job at an organization with more than a thousand employees. It was a step up, but soon Lisa was hearing the old voices in her head: "She doesn't understand HR," and "I don't have to be treated like this." Lisa says,

"Everything at this new job was different—the field, the company, the mission, the people—the only thing that was the same was me."

Lisa was getting in her own way, and she knew it, so she contacted the leadership coach from her old job. Over a period of several years, the coach helped her to recognize her hot buttons and consciously decide not to engage with colleagues while feeling upset or defensive. Lisa achieved a higher level of confidence and leadership ability and gained influence with her colleagues and supervisors. She is now better able to keep work in perspective and is a better wife and mother because she doesn't bring her frustrations home.

Lisa credits her coach, whom she keeps on speed dial, with these positive changes. However, the process was never easy. "Self-development is tough work. It's messy and painful but the insights are worth it and will move you ahead by leaps and bounds," she says. "And once you've made a leap forward, you won't be able to leave things as they are. You'll be compelled to make a change and the status quo will no longer be acceptable to you. Coaching is the best gift you can give yourself."

Lisa's favorable attitude toward coaching has become commonplace in today's business world. As they reported in *Fast Company* in 2006, Jim Bolt and Brian Underhill conducted a study that found that 56 percent of surveyed companies emphasized coaching as a major learning method, and two years later, 51 percent of the same organizations said that the use of coaching had increased. The investigators also discovered that coaching was no longer a "fix-it tool" for leaders with problems and was instead being used to help high-potential leaders get even better.

In fact, at the time of the second study, 43 percent of CEOs and 71 percent of senior team members in the surveyed organizations had worked with a coach. Sixty-three percent of the companies said they planned to increase their use of coaching over the following five years, and an incredible 92 percent of coached leaders said they planned to engage a coach again.

If you think that getting a coach is a good move for you, you're probably right. Your first step should be to contact your human resources department to see what resources may be available to you for free. You can also ask your manager or a trusted mentor. Those who work in smaller organizations may find that no coaching infrastructure is in place, but that shouldn't deter you. Ask around for a referral or find one through the International Coach Federation (www.coachfederation.org). Before you sign on, review the best coaching practices on the ICF's website to ensure that your coach is qualified and that you know what to expect from the process. Interview your prospective coach or ask for a trial session first so that you can determine if he is someone with whom you feel comfortable and challenged.

Of course, it's not enough to hire a coach—you have to make the most of the relationship. Give coaching the time and attention it deserves, and set concrete goals with your coach as quickly as possible so that you can begin feeling a sense of accomplishment. Don't shy away from discomfort, and keep the lines of communication open so that your coach can help you work through emotional roadblocks that may arise. Also, don't forget to keep your boss involved. Alert her to the areas you're working on and check in periodically to see if she's noticing improvement. You can gain valuable insights from peers and direct reports as well—ask your coach to assist you in developing anonymous feedback surveys for them.

As the majority of coaching engagements last between six and twelve months, you and your coach should work together to determine an appropriate end point. If a coach has done his job well, then you won't be dependent on him and will be able to continue working effectively on your own.

In addition to coaching, psychotherapy is a viable alternative for individuals who experience distress in a series of jobs. I believe that most people can benefit from therapy, and just because you could use the assistance now doesn't mean you'll be chained to a therapist's office for life. Like effective coaching, the best psychotherapy is time limited, and sometimes a stint can be as short as two or three visits.

The type of therapy that's most helpful for the issues I've talked about in this chapter is cognitive-behavioral therapy, or CBT. Extensively studied, CBT focuses on maladaptive thinking patterns and beliefs. With the help of a trained therapist, the client is encouraged to monitor and write down destructive thoughts and attempt to rationalize why they are false. CBT is well suited for people who want to actively participate in their own recovery and has been shown to be useful in psychological problems ranging from depression to eating disorders. You can search for qualified professionals at the Association for Behavioral and Cognitive Therapies (www.abct.org) and the Academy of Cognitive Therapy (www.academyofct.org) websites.

If seeking the services of a professional coach or therapist isn't for you, you might consider engaging a role model who gets along well in the work environment in which you're having trouble.

"Look for someone you would like to emulate behaviorally," says Leigh Steere, a career counselor. "The ideal person handles difficult situations with aplomb, demonstrates strong leadership, and is successful in her profession. Talk to her about specific skills you'd like to acquire and see if she'd be willing to mentor you on them. Define what this would involve, and then listen closely to the wisdom she provides in your time together."

MYTHBUSTER'S SUMMARY

- People who can't or won't take responsibility for the role they play in difficult workplace encounters rarely achieve high levels of success. Instead of searching in vain for the perfect work situation, take a look at yourself and determine how you can change things from the inside out.

- You can prevent a bad attitude by taking control of automatic negative thoughts. When confronted with an unfair or anger-producing situation, analyze whether the situation is objectively as bad as it seems.

- Beware of irrational expectations. Instead of insisting that something *should* happen, rephrase it as something you *would like* to happen and how you are going to cope if it doesn't happen.

- Emotional intelligence is an underrated but critical set of skills. Improve your EQ at work by planning for stressful or upsetting situations in advance, paying attention to the signs that you're losing control over your emotions, and monitoring nonverbal cues.

■ If you've experienced distress in a series of jobs and are unsure of the next step to take, consider employing a qualified coach or psychotherapist. Select a professional with whom you feel comfortable but challenged.

You Won't Get Laid Off; You're Too Essential

like all career advisers, I often tell people that they should aim to be indispensable at their jobs. The truth is, though, that today more than ever company loyalty is a thing of the past, and while consistently trying to add value to your organization is a good move, sometimes it isn't enough. Randall Barker, a vice president of human resources at A Plus Benefits (www .aplusbenefits.com), sums it up this way: "If you really think you cannot be replaced, you'd better update your resume because reality is speeding toward you like a fifty-caliber bullet."

Why is the myth of indispensability still so rampant in a postrecession business world? Jay Meschke, president of EFL Associates (www.cbiz.com), an executive search firm, believes it's because employees confuse the good work they're doing in their role with the organization's bigger picture. "Sure, the employee's work may be crucial to her manager and the short-term objectives of that division, but what if that division isn't contributing financially to the organization as a whole?" he says. "Or what if the employee's business unit is not integral to the holistic success of the company and unrelated to its future?"

Adds Bettina Seidman, president of executive coaching firm SEIDBET Associates (www.seidbet.com), "In my view, many employees do not understand the downsizing and layoff process. Because it is based on financial issues, often entire departments or sectors are downsized. A percentage of payroll needs to be cut and good employees are impacted as well as less competent employees. Even a great relationship with your manager may not save you."

If anyone in the magazine world was viewed to be indispensable, it was Ruth Reichl. The personable, raven-haired editor in chief of *Gourmet* magazine began writing about food in 1972, when she published *Mmmmm: A Feastiary.* As co-owner and chef of the Swallow Restaurant in the mid-1970s, Ruth gathered the practical experience she'd need for the restaurant critic stints that followed at *New West* magazine, *California* magazine, and the *Los Angeles Times.* Eventually moving on to the *New York Times* in 1993 and then *Gourmet* in 1999, Ruth authored several bestselling memoirs, including *Tender at the Bone* and *Comfort Me with Apples.*

According to the *New York Times*'s Media Decoder blog, *Gourmet* became "a magazine of almost biblical status in the food world," and Ruth was its Eve. By the early 2000s, she'd been honored with multiple industry awards for her work in food journalism and restaurant criticism. In 2009, despite the recession, she led *Gourmet* to its highest circulation numbers in the magazine's sixty-nine-year history and signed on several new advertisers.

Nevertheless, in the fall of 2009, *Gourmet*'s parent company, Condé Nast, announced that it would close *Gourmet* due to a lack of profitable advertising and a poor economy. "These businesses should be 25 percent net margin businesses," chief executive Charles H. Townsend told the *New York Times*. "Some of our businesses, like *Gourmet*, cost us money to run and have slipped into the red. We will not be in that position after today. We won't have businesses that don't make a contribution."

Condé Nast laid off most of *Gourmet*'s employees—including Ruth Reichl. It was speculated that Condé Nast would find another place in its empire for an editor as valuable as Ruth, but this didn't happen. She was forced to pack up her office along with the rest of her staff.

If it can happen to someone with as powerful a resume as Ruth Reichl, it can happen to you. How can you protect yourself? Your best weapon is to let go of the myth, because believing in your own indispensability can actually hurt you. You must understand the real reasons behind organizational layoffs, learn to recognize the signs that a layoff is pending, and, if you've made some missteps, do a course correction to avoid being fired. This chapter will cover all of these subjects, and it will also address how to cope productively in the unfortunate event that you are let go.

The Real Reasons behind Corporate Layoffs

Roberta Matuson of Northampton, Massachusetts, graduated from college in the early 1980s, a time when jobs for business and human resources management majors were scarce. Roberta moved to Houston and picked up some HR experience in retail before interviewing for a job in her dream industry, the oil field business. "I was able to break in, and right away the financial benefits were substantial," she says.

Roberta did everything she could to impress her new employer. "I was a sponge," she says. "I worked on whatever projects my boss gave me and spent many an evening at my desk, brainstorming ways to prove my worth. I was always volunteering to help my peers, and I developed a great reputation as a team player."

It was all any twenty-something employee could hope for. But the oil industry was in trouble. Profits plummeted and Roberta's company rumbled about layoffs. Despite the fact that everyone who worked with her loved her, Roberta learned early on that she would be a casualty. "The senior people in my department explained that in these types of situations, the company will keep the employees who are capable of doing more than just their own jobs. At that point, I only had two years of HR experience and was no match for the people with fifteen-plus years under their belts."

Roberta doesn't hold her layoff against the company, but being let go as a high performer did instill in her a certain distrust. "I work for myself now, because I believe that's the only way I can truly control my future," she says. Now fifty-one years old, Roberta is hoping that sharing her workplace experiences in the book *Suddenly in Charge! Managing Up, Managing Down and Succeeding All Around* will help others who find themselves in similar situations.

Few organizations escaped the global recession of the late 2000s unscathed. The domino effect started with an individual who, receiving less money from her employer, decided to reduce the amount of money she spent. A company that provided her with products or services suffered from the smaller revenue and was forced to carry more debt. Its overhead, personnel, and operations costs stayed the same, but suddenly it didn't have enough funds coming in to pay them. The company's leaders tried to cut expenses and increase sales, but their efforts were not sufficient. Since acquisition was not an option and the company didn't want to declare bankruptcy or go out of business, the company had to downsize.

Even postrecession, downsizing is a reality for many organizations. Once the decision to downsize is made, a company has the option of selling a unit or division or laying off employees. Many companies choose the latter simply because it's easier and allows them to continue running business operations with minimal disruption. The question then becomes: who do we terminate? The layoff must be done in a way that appears fair to all involved.

Many companies select people to lay off based on seniority, which does make sense. After all, tenured employees have more experience with their individual jobs as well as with the company as a whole. The company has invested more time training and supporting them. I sometimes see, however, that the situation is the other way around. A company may lay off older employees because younger ones are cheaper and aren't likely to retire anytime soon.

Other times companies will lay off groups of workers in product or service areas that are unprofitable, or they will let go of workers with job functions that are redundant with those of other employees on staff. It is generally considered less risky to lay off entire departments than single employees, but some companies leave layoffs to the discretion of the individual manager. In this case, suggests Jay Meschke, troublemakers will be pegged immediately. "Employees who are perceived to be high maintenance or possess less than positive attitudes or results will be the first to go," he says.

When Being Indispensable Has the Opposite Effect

But regardless of the real reasons behind layoffs, being indispensable can't hurt you . . . or can it? Business consultant Marc Lawn (www.thebusinessgp.com) thinks so. "In my experience, the indispensable employee believes he is always right," he says. "He rules the roost and is considered the 'go to' person. He's blind to anything being his fault and may even get to the point of bragging that he's so critical to the business that he cannot be removed."

Lawn has also found that people who consider themselves indispensable get easily hurt when people don't consult them on projects, mistakenly believing that the business revolves around and cannot run without their input. They also get mired in the details, sometimes preferring to own areas that aren't truly important or that others don't care about. And because they are so efficient at doing their jobs well while maintaining the status quo, they tend to block necessary progress within the organization. This lethal combination of traits actually makes indispensable people more vulnerable to dismissal.

Lawn has seen it firsthand. He tells the story of Claire, a woman who worked for him while he was employed at a $2 billion consumer goods company. "We had an internal design studio and Claire was the best designer we had by a long shot, and she got to thinking she was indispensable," he says. "She'd been with the company for thirteen years, but when we decided to outsource the department, she proved very inflexible. Claire could not adapt to the new system and apply her skills to other roles in the business, and she was eventually let go."

Recognizing a Pending Layoff—and Taking Action

Most people prefer being laid off to being fired because it's easier to rationalize. Usually, it's less personal and there's nothing you can do about it, right? This is often true, but there are ways to prepare for it and perhaps prevent it, starting with recognizing the signs that a company-wide layoff may be headed your way. For example:

- **Your company has a new CEO who has been brought on to improve the company's results.** One of the first things he'll probably do to make his mark is "trim the fat."

- **Wall Street says your company hasn't hit its financial targets.** This may mean that particular divisions are underperforming and changes will be made.

- **MSNBC, CNN, and the industry blogs are buzzing about your company.** The prospect of layoffs may or may not be mentioned, but as they say, "no news is good news."

- **The company has officially tightened its belt.** Budgets are being cut left and right, the training course you wanted to take is no longer being offered, and the expense policy memo was just sent out *again*.

- **Senior executives are disappearing into conference rooms for long periods of time.** They could be planning a reorganization of the company's workforce, a development that often results in layoffs.

Take a moment to think about the current climate of your organization. Have you noticed any of the above signs, or other red flags that concern you? Write your observations here.

_____

_____

_____

_____

Conscientious employees are so busy working that sometimes they don't pay attention to what's going on around them. This is a mistake, because the indicators above are pretty reliable, and if one or more of them is occurring in your company, it's in your best interest to take action before you find yourself out of a job. This book is full of suggestions for networking with the right people, making yourself more marketable, and updating your resume with your current skills and accomplishments—take advantage of them now so that you have less legwork to do later.

You might be familiar with competitors that do the same work as your current company and are having fewer financial difficulties. You might subtly put out feelers to see if they are hiring. Do not feel guilty about this. You can rest assured the company is taking care of itself in deciding who to lay off. If you don't look out for you, no one else will.

Understandably, those facing a potential layoff are concerned about their finances. A cushy severance package may not be a reality for you, so read this book's guidance on anticipating a loss of income (see chapter 10), and have a look at your company's employment handbook to determine how you might transfer your health insurance and retirement plans.

If you sense the ship is going down, you can also search for a lifeboat. Changing roles is one approach. If the bulk of your job involves an initiative that's coming to an end, for instance, you might try jumping onto a new project before the company needs to find something else for you to do. You could also apply to work with a group that is currently understaffed, although, as I've covered, there can be danger in becoming the least tenured person in a department.

If an internal move is not an option, look for ways to improve your performance in the job you have. "Always be on the lookout for a better way to use time, streamline a procedure, or shave costs," says Bettina Seidman. "Prioritize your work according to the core mission of the business." Don't gossip or whine about layoffs with your co-workers—if you must vent, rely on a trusted friend or family member outside the company. And stay busy so that your managers can't complain about a lack of focus or productivity.

Make sure you're on top of announcements and chatter that reflect changes in strategic direction, and continue to nourish your relationships with senior managers who have the ear of the company's top executives. "Employees at companies in trouble should follow the money and latch on to individuals with perceived power. These could be the fast-rising management star or the most profitable client," says Jay Meschke.

Your company might try to avoid a layoff by asking employees to take furlough days, work part-time, or telecommute. Working a part-time job instead of a full-time job is an unreasonable financial proposition for many, so you would need to decide if it's worth it to keep this job until the storm has passed. It may be more realistic to give up perks like stock options or a gym membership, and you should be first in line to take advantage of the opportunity to work from home. This kind of solution is a win-win. Your company gets to save money on real estate and overhead and you'll be more efficient without the daily commute.

Once you've done everything you can, try not to worry. You don't want to lose sleep and damage your health by being constantly stressed that a layoff is around the corner. All you can do is prepare to the best of your ability, and then let the cards fall where they may. Give yourself a pep talk every morning so that your confidence stays high. After all, what's the worst that can happen? You will be laid off, and because you'll have lots of company, future employers would probably not hold it against you.

How to Stave Off a Firing

While writing this book, I met a guy named Sebastian at a conference. Sebastian told me that he had worked as an activity director at a Florida-based family resort for the last few years and that his boss had recently told him that the staff and the members didn't like him. Sebastian did not understand this feedback. He had just circulated a membership evaluation form that rated him an above-average 4 out of 5. Additionally, he had had no verbal exchanges with any staff members to indicate that they were unhappy with him, and certainly no one had filed a complaint. Sebastian confided that he was insecure because he didn't know where this attack from his boss was coming from, and he was worried he might be fired.

Just a few months before the conversation with his boss, Sebastian probably would have told me that as one of the highest-rated staff members, he was indispensable. This situation took him completely by surprise, and he was right to be concerned about it. The fact that his boss was looking for excuses to complain about him indicated to me that there was—literally—trouble in paradise. In a subsequent conversation with him, I learned that Sebastian's boss had recently documented the fact that Sebastian had overspent his budget. Neither of us was particularly surprised when he was fired a few months later.

Like Sebastian, you may have received signs that your demise is imminent. These could include:

- Your performance review wasn't stellar, and/or you are on probation.

- You were hired for a specific project and that project wasn't done well or at all.

- You are always clashing with your boss over nonissues.

- Your boss has told you that you need to change your attitude.

- Your boss is keeping a paper trail by documenting every conversation in e-mail.

- Your colleagues are handling responsibilities that were formerly yours.

- Your colleagues have stopped confiding in you.

- You have been vocal about your unhappiness in the organization.

- Meetings are being held without you.

- HR has spoken to you about inappropriate behavior (emotional outbursts, insubordination, sexual harassment, etc.).

- An important client or partner has said she no longer wishes to work with you.

Based on these suggestions, write down any warning signs that your job may be in jeopardy.

_____

_____

_____

_____

Just because one or more of these signs applies doesn't definitively mean you will lose your job. Most organizations—and managers—are somewhat tolerant of employees who are going through a hard time. They may well have faith that you will work through your issues. However, it's important to understand when you're in danger of being fired so that you can take steps to avert it—because unlike layoffs, many firings can be prevented.

If you're on probation related to poor performance, any actions your boss instructed you to take should be burned into your brain. Do whatever it takes to improve in each documented area within a matter of weeks. If the feedback is that you are not contributing, you should zealously amp up your performance in ways that can be measured and that tangibly affect the organization's bottom line. For example, after the meeting with his boss, Sebastian might have implemented a member-requested surfing class, which would bring in additional revenue for the resort and boost his customer satisfaction ratings.

You should also build up a unique set of skills and take ultra-specific training courses so that no current employee can do your job as well as you can and the organization would have to hire someone new. Stay in the spotlight—in a good way—so that your absence would be glaringly obvious. While they still aren't indispensable, highly visible, highly specialized employees are much more trouble to replace.

If you've gotten in hot water with your boss or HR for inappropriate behavior, you might still save your job provided you stop the behavior right away and sincerely apologize to all involved. You might, for example, say something like: "I know I really screwed up. I want you to know that I've learned a lot from this experience, and I promise that nothing like it will ever happen again." Be honest with yourself. Have you done something that has made you unpopular around the office, even if it's as harmless as a gossip session gone bad? You'll need to turn things around as quickly as possible. Go out of your way to help your co-workers with their projects. Arrange to have the whole department sign a card for the assistant who has been out sick. Organize Friday Happy Hour and pay for the first round of drinks. As I've talked about in previous chapters, being the employee that everyone likes will make you less vulnerable.

Speaking of being liked, things get a little dicey when you haven't done anything wrong, but for whatever reason your boss has a negative perception of you or your work. His dislike may be unwarranted—perhaps you look like the neighbor with whom he has a bitter relationship; or it may be semiwarranted—perhaps he recognizes your talent and is worried you'll end up with his job. Regardless, if you live in an at-will state, your boss doesn't officially need a reason to fire you and can do so with minimal justification, simply because he doesn't like you.

In the event that you enjoy your job and want to keep it, you will have to confront your boss. Swallow your pride and be prepared to be the bigger man or woman, unfair as the situation may be. Set up a meeting and say something like: "I'm concerned that I'm not meeting your expectations. What can I do to improve things?" If his problem with you is truly personal, you may shock him into making it less obvious.

If he defends himself by calling out your performance, calmly ask him for examples by saying: "Thanks for the feedback. Would you mind sharing some specific instances so that I can start moving in the right direction?" For instance, Sebastian might have asked his boss to share what members have said—and in what context—to indicate that they don't like him. Pay close attention to any documentation that is supplied. This is a good way to assess the case your boss is building against you. Hopefully this meeting will result in some type of resolution, which you should recount via e-mail for paper trail purposes. If it doesn't, you could try the last-ditch approach of talking to a senior manager or an HR representative. I say last-ditch because going over your boss's head could cause a simmering situation to explode outright, so you want to be sure you've explored all other options. When approaching someone in HR or management, be solicitous and nondefensive. The perception should be that you are only having the conversation because you want to effectively correct course. For instance, instead of saying, "Kim has a problem with me and nothing I do seems to make her happy," you might offer, "I've gotten some feedback from Kim that I'd like to run by you so that I can continue to perform to the best of my ability."

Here's a trick you see a lot in Hollywood movies. If you're 90 percent sure you're about to be fired, you could resign first. This approach has advantages and disadvantages. The advantages are that you won't have to tell future employers that you were fired, you get the last word, and you might actually ease the tension between you and your boss by doing his dirty work for him. The disadvantages are mostly financial—the company may not pay severance or continue your benefits as long as it would have if you had been fired.

As a mother, I'd be remiss if I left the firing topic without mentioning a key risk factor, and that's pregnancy. Although we're lucky to have the Pregnancy Discrimination Act, which states that employers can't refuse to hire a woman because she is pregnant, can't fire her for being pregnant, and can't treat her differently because of her pregnancy, the truth is that employers disregard the law every day by attempting to get rid of pregnant employees. Why would they do such a thing? The cost of medical benefits and family leave is one reason, and concern for company welfare is another. From the employer's perspective, a woman might not return from maternity leave, and even if she does, she might be less effective at her job once she has a child to worry about.

What's the solution? First, don't tell your boss you're pregnant until it's physically impossible to hide it. Second, stay alert to signs of discrimination. If they appear, nip the situation in the bud right away. Tell your boss you feel that you're being treated unfairly because you're pregnant, and put it in writing. Having these claims out in the open will make your boss nervous about future legal action and will cause him to backpedal—which could very well save your job.

How to Handle Being Fired

Before he was a radio host, John Donald "Don" Imus Jr. was raised on an Arizona cattle ranch, served as a bugler in the Marine Corps, and was brakeman on the Southern Pacific Railroad. One day in 1968, after hearing a morning radio DJ, Don convinced the owner of California radio station KUTY to hire him. He went on to work as a DJ at WGAR in Cleveland, and in 1971 he landed at WNBC in New York, the top radio market in the world. His show, *Imus in the Morning*, was advertised alongside the famous program of his colleague and rival Howard Stern.

Starting in 1993, *Imus in the Morning* was nationally syndicated, and in 1996, it was simulcast on MSNBC, featuring a rough-and-ready Don Imus donning a cowboy hat. Part of Don's appeal was his appetite for controversy. He never hesitated to put people down if he felt they deserved it, calling Rush Limbaugh a "fat, pill-popping loser" and television journalist Lesley Stahl a "gutless, lying weasel."

One day in April 2007, however, Don went too far. While discussing the NCAA Women's Basketball Championship, Don referred to the Rutgers players as "rough girls" and "nappy-headed hos." The public was outraged at what they perceived as racial slurs, and Don issued an apology. As a guest on Al Sharpton's radio talk show, *Keepin' It Real*, Don said, "Our agenda is to be funny, and sometimes we go too far. And this time we went way too far. Here's what I've learned: you can't make fun of everybody, because some people don't deserve it."

Nevertheless, Al Sharpton called for Don to be fired, and after much internal and external debate, *Imus in the Morning* was canceled. Just hours after he'd learned he'd been fired, Don met with Rutgers women's basketball coach C. Vivian Stringer and her players at the New Jersey governor's mansion. Stringer commented that the meeting went well and said that her team had accepted Don's apology. "He came to the meeting in spite of the fact that he lost his job, and we have to give him credit for that," she said at the time.

Regardless of what you think of Don Imus personally, or whether you feel that these remarks warranted his show's cancellation, you can't argue with the fact that he handled his firing gracefully and with tact and dignity.

Because your behavior after bad news has a bearing on your career reputation as a whole, this should be your approach as well. The first thing you should do after being fired is leave the building. Immediately. Organizations sometimes have just-fired employees escorted out right away in order to protect their assets. If this is the case, don't make a scene—just go. Schedule a follow-up meeting the next day to talk specifics and sign your paperwork and to return to your office to collect your belongings.

Even if you haven't been officially escorted out, no good can come of remaining in your office after receiving this news. Tell your boss you are taking the rest of the day to absorb it and then go home and do just that. Call a family member or friend, take a walk in the park, or watch your favorite TV show—whatever helps you get through. Allow yourself to be upset because you are a human being and this is an upsetting occurrence.

When you do return to the office for your last day(s), keep your cool. Take deep breaths before you walk in and tell yourself that an emotional outburst will only make things worse. Don't complain about the situation or the company to your colleagues or argue with your boss. And for the love of God, don't threaten to sue anyone. This is exactly the type of comment that could be passed on—and received as poison by—future employers. Pack up your office neatly, clean up your computer and other company-owned electronic devices, and take only the things that you own and work product that you personally created.

During the closing meeting with your boss and/or the human resources department, benefits should be your chief priority. Can you apply for unemployment? Are you eligible for severance? How much will it be, and what conditions have to be in place to get it? How long can you continue receiving the company's health insurance and what should you do after that? How should you transfer your retirement plan?

Also inquire about how to tie up loose ends with the company—returning materials you might have at home, briefing colleagues, saying good-bye to clients, etc. Find out if you are eligible to be rehired at some point, and if there is any outplacement assistance available to you now. Maintain a professional tone throughout this discussion. If your departure involves an official exit interview, try to be as constructive as possible and keep the vitriol to a minimum. Remember that the goal is to leave on good terms so that you will receive as many benefits as possible, and perhaps even a positive reference. Plus, you never know if you will be in a position to work with this company—or the individuals in it—again. Even if you feel angry and betrayed now, you want to leave your options open.

If you think you were fired illegally, don't do anything rash. Instead, peruse the U.S. Equal Employment Opportunity Commission (www.eeoc.gov) and the U.S. Department of Labor (www.dol.gov) websites and/or consult with an employment lawyer (www.lawyers.com) to determine if a law has in fact been broken. Realize, though, that this is rare, and that even if you do have a case, it will be expensive and stressful to take it to court. You may be better off just moving on to another job.

Speaking of which, when interviewing, don't bad-mouth your former employer. Rather than blaming your boss or citing a personality conflict, be straightforward about the problems in the company or your department that led to your firing while taking responsibility for your role in the situation.

When You Can't Control It, It May Be for the Best

From 1996 to 2006, a group of academic researchers went onsite at Boeing to study what happens when a company is inundated with layoffs. As they recount in their resulting book, *Turbulence: Boeing and the State of American Workers and Managers*, the researchers found that laid-off employees were actually better off than the ones who stayed behind and struggled to stay relevant and visible and hold on to their jobs.

The scientists, who included Edward Greenberg, Leon Grunberg, Sarah Moore, and Patricia Sikora, interviewed 3,500 Boeing employees at all levels as the company was in the process of merging with McDonnell Douglas and downsizing its workforce by 33 percent. As Michelle Conlin reported in a 2009 *Business Week* article, "With each round of layoffs, the survivors hustled to reinvent themselves. They re-proved, re-auditioned, and repositioned, only to watch yet another new manager—pushing the fad du jour—parade through the door." Human resources specialist Frank Zemek described to Conlin the survivors' guilt, the intense stress of not knowing if and when the hatchet was going to fall, the numbness and disengagement, and the deep, pervasive grief of managers who had fired people.

The researchers discovered that overall, the employees who were laid off from Boeing were happier than those who stayed. Employees who remained at the company were twice as depressed and more likely to suffer from insomnia, alcohol abuse, and chronic health complaints.

So if you've been laid off or fired, take heart. It may be a blessing in disguise. You can now feel free to look for a new job that you're more excited about, among managers and colleagues who appreciate your talents, where you won't have to do the work of three people to earn the same paycheck.

MYTHBUSTER'S SUMMARY

- While consistently trying to add value to your organization is a good move, sometimes it isn't enough. Because layoffs are often based on the company's overall financial health, they affect good employees as well as less competent employees.

- People who consider themselves indispensable mistakenly believe that the business revolves around and cannot run without their input. And because they are so efficient at maintaining the status quo, they tend to block necessary progress and are actually more vulnerable to dismissal.

- If word on the street says there will be layoffs, sniff out competitors who do similar work and are in better financial straits, pursue an internal move to a profitable department, and nurture your relationships with senior executives.

- If your boss doesn't like you, it doesn't matter how good you are—your job is in jeopardy. Tell your boss you're concerned that you aren't meeting his or her expectations and ask what you can do to improve the relationship.

- In the event that you are let go, handle the news with tact and dignity, because your behavior may affect your future career and reputation.

If Only You Could Leave Corporate America, Your Career Would Be Perfect

Thirty-year-old Aaron Patzer has made a mint. Literally. In 2006, the former IBM engineer founded Mint.com, a piece of online personal finance software that allows users to track bank, credit card, investment, and loan transactions and balances through a single user interface. In addition to building the alpha version of Mint himself, Aaron created a team of thirty-five professionals to launch the software. He raised $31 million in funding from venture capital funds and angel investors and grew revenues in excess of 400 percent.

Aaron won accolades from a half dozen media sources, including *Money* magazine's personal finance award and *Fortune*'s "40 Executives under 40" award, before selling Mint.com to Intuit, a global accounting software firm, for an incredible $170 million in

November 2009. By anyone's definition, Aaron was a successful entrepreneur. And yet he did not choose to make another "mint" by starting a second business. Instead, he joined Intuit as the general manager for the company's personal finance group. "As the founder of a start-up, I operated in a state of paranoia, thinking that every day could be my last," he explains. "When you work for an established organization, you have so many more resources. You have the freedom to think about the bigger things—like how you can expand globally and how you can innovate."

In his new role, Aaron oversees a division of one hundred people and $100 million in revenue, as well as product, marketing, and new business strategy. Despite his entrepreneurial success, Aaron chose to return to the corporate world, and he couldn't be happier. "I'm learning so much about different industries and job functions, and I see so many opportunities for my career. I feel that the experience I'm getting puts me in a position to go anywhere I want, from a CEO job at a medium-sized organization to a general manager job at any Fortune 500 company."

Over the last few years—ever since the economy tanked in late 2008—there has been a major push toward entrepreneurship. A 2009 survey by FindLaw.com indicates that 61 percent of Americans have either started or thought about starting a small business. Why? Well, for a long time companies were losing their shirts and people were getting laid off or fired in droves, and those that were left behind were often forced to do the work of three employees. "People are fearful of the future now," adds Richard Reyes, a business and finance coach (www.thefinancialqb.com). "We are looking for more certainty and, at the same time, are constantly being bombarded by media and government criticizing the greedy business owner. We convince ourselves that the best way to have a great future is to break out of corporate America and do it on our own."

I understand this. Really, I do. It makes sense why your dad, your roommate, and every career adviser on the planet have told you to forget the corporate b.s. and go work for yourself. Most authors are on board too. Lately it seems like every business book I pick up is written by a successful entrepreneur who either (a) experienced a ridiculous amount of trial and tribulation to pursue his dream—such as living homeless for a year—or (b) shunned a traditional education and drove a high-powered career on resourcefulness alone.

I wondered aloud one day why these stories are so appealing, even though they are so frequently published they are almost a cliché, and my husband reminded me that they represent the American dream and the fact that we exist in a society where anything is possible, and just by virtue of living here, we can achieve whatever we put our minds to. But does this hold true today?

Forgive me for sounding like a wet blanket, but I prefer to be more of a realist. Today, it's fashionable to say that you're going to become an entrepreneur, that you'll shun the corporate world to go out and start a business according to your own values and your own rules. But here's the thing. Running a business is harder than it looks, and the idea that entrepreneurship is the best solution for everyone is a myth. Not only is being an entrepreneur costly, nerve-wracking, and incredibly hard work, but because of the way our economy is structured, it's simply impossible for everyone to be one.

It's also worth nothing that corporate America isn't as bad a place as it used to be. Don't forget what I've been saying all along, which is that many organizations have thrown out bloody politics with the recessionary bathwater and are earnestly trying to create more honest, humane workplaces that extol the very values you would pursue working for yourself. This chapter will explore the real story behind entrepreneurship, and why it may not be the right solution for you. I'll talk about the personality traits that are essential if you want to be self-employed and explain why office politics don't go away once you leave corporate America. Then I'll discuss why many people are better off working in the corporate world, including the three little Ps—peace, prestige, and perks. I'll close with a discussion of intrapreneurship, which is a strategy that allows you to have the best of both worlds.

Realities of Entrepreneurship

Marian Gordon, who describes herself as "fifty-five years young," is a lifelong New Yorker, raised in Brooklyn and Queens. She started her career at the age of seventeen while attending Queens College and Pace University at night. Marian's first employer was SESAC, a music copyright company, and she quickly grew restless. "I realized that I was too young to advance to a top position and thought I could make more money on my own," she says. "A lot of my friends were starting companies, so I decided to do the same. In addition to the income, I looked forward to greater flexibility and more vacation time."

Marian's friend joined her in opening a screen-printing factory. "Her position was sales and mine was production, but unfortunately she didn't produce any sales and I ended up doing everything," she says. "The first five years I was in business, I worked far too hard for far too little money. Good help was extremely hard to find, payroll taxes and insurance were expensive, and I had to play therapist to employees, customers, and vendors to get what I wanted out of them."

Marian's accountant told her that she might as well be working at McDonald's for the money she was making in relation to the hours she was putting in. "Not that there's anything wrong with working for McDonald's, but it wasn't what I was expecting. I was too busy trying to make sales and produce orders to pay attention to the little things. I paid my taxes late and the penalties and interest killed me."

Marian purchased another business and consolidated her existing venture with the new one. "I quickly got dragged down by extra expenses, old equipment, and unnecessary employees," she remembers. "Even though I did my due diligence, the previous owners provided false information regarding their customers and accounts. I held on for three years, but then had to shut down."

Marian never imagined that starting and maintaining her business would be so much more difficult than remaining in the traditional business world. "I didn't really think about it, and I didn't get good enough advice," she says.

Marian is not alone. I meet someone every week who says he has a fabulous business idea. He'll say something vague about how he hates his job and thinks he can make a ton of money off this new product. Usually I'll try to explain that if you want to start a company, the motivation fueled by being bored with your work or hating your boss won't be enough. You'll have to think hard about the unmet marketplace need your product or service addresses, and you must learn how to uncover and employ the right mix of resources to further your cause.

Then you will need to undertake the many tasks associated with getting a new business off the ground. "The biggest hardship of being an entrepreneur is that everything falls on you," says Richard Reyes, echoing Marian's experience. "It falls on you to produce your product, it falls on you to supervise production, it falls on you to market that product, it falls on you to sell that product, it falls on you to deliver that product, and it falls on you to make sure you make a profit."

As Marian learned, the financial implications of having your own business are not to be underestimated. "It falls on you to make sure that all the bills and any employees are paid," continues Reyes. "And finally, it falls on you to make sure that all the little things that add absolutely nothing to the bottom line—but cost a lot—are taken care of, like insurance, licenses, city and state filings, accounting and bookkeeping, and dealing with regulators."

As Mark Herschberg, CEO of White Knight Consulting (www.whiteknightconsulting.com) puts it, if you're a good software developer, you'll be able to get a job as a software developer. But being a good software developer doesn't mean you have what it takes to run a software development company. "If you're not up to dealing with all the other aspects of running a business— from designing and manufacturing to hiring and marketing— entrepreneurship may not be the right fit for you," he says.

Having a business is a twenty-four/seven job no matter how small or large your company is, and you're on the job every moment of every day. An entrepreneur has to be willing to do whatever it takes for the benefit of the business. "It's like being responsible for a family," says Herschberg. "You have to suck things up, like driving all night to solve a customer's problem and paying your employees before you get paid yourself."

Entrepreneurship also brings a much greater risk of failure and a much greater risk that people won't support what you're trying to do. "When Lehman Brothers failed, 99 percent of the employees had little or no responsibility for that outcome," says Herschberg. "When it's your company and it goes under, the responsibility is on you. Your livelihood directly depends on your actions, and if you have employees, their livelihood depends on those actions too." Naysayers are a challenge too. "People aren't going to understand your vision, why you're leaving a steady paycheck, and why you want their funding. You'll hear many more nos than yeses," Herschberg adds.

Some people think they can circumvent these thorny issues by becoming sole proprietors, or those who work by themselves and contract their services to a variety of employers. This is different from an entrepreneur, who launches a business that involves other people. I chose the path of sole proprietorship because I didn't have the nerve to pursue entrepreneurship full throttle. By becoming an independent consultant, I could choose my own assignments and customize my schedule.

The amount of stress in my sole proprietorship scenario, however, has been significant. I always need to be thinking about the next job. If I don't get out there and hustle, I don't get paid. I can never stop thinking about how to generate business; even when I'm en route to Jamaica on vacation I'm determining whether the stranger in the seat next to me is a promising prospect. And planning large purchases and retirement funding is more difficult because I can't be sure of my income in a given year.

Being a sole proprietor doesn't give you as much control over your day as you might think. There will be times when you are forced to take on a job that you don't want to do because you need the money. You will have clients who try to take advantage of you, and others who refuse to pay you. Because you'll pay most of your own expenses, you'll have to be much more careful about the money you spend on your work (supplies, travel, etc.) than you would if you had a company's backing. Unless you hire an assistant, you'll spend much more time engaged in administrative activity, and your taxes will be exponentially more complicated.

As you no doubt gather, being an entrepreneur or a sole proprietor requires a certain personality. Let's look at the traits that are essential to be content working for yourself.

Personality Traits of the Self-Employed

When I think about the self-employed people I know, one word comes to mind first: confident. Herschberg agrees. "Being an entrepreneur means rolling the dice and betting on yourself and your vision," he says. "If you don't believe in yourself, no one else will."

Entrepreneurs and sole proprietors are business savvy and intuitively understand what their customers need and want. They're passionate, optimistic, resourceful, and full of energy. Their self-discipline is off the charts. And this is very important—they're outgoing and social. It's up to the entrepreneur or sole proprietor to make herself visible. "The average plumber, graphic designer, or marketing consultant has to be out there constantly, reminding people that she provides this specific service and is available," says Herschberg. Along these same lines, if you work for yourself, you must be an excellent salesperson. "Even if you have employees to help with sales, they will never have as much vested in the process as you do, so you are the person most likely to bring in the deals."

People with thin skins don't last very long working for themselves. "As an entrepreneur, you need to speak with gravitas or else your team and your clients will walk all over you," says Herschberg. "There will be times when you have to make an executive decision, speak firmly and persuasively, and get everyone aligned." And finally, entrepreneurs and sole proprietors are comfortable relying on themselves for answers. Even if they're scared, they push past the fear. Rather than waiting for someone to tell them what to do, they're proactive and jump at opportunities without second-guessing themselves.

Kellie Auld, a human resources professional who lives in the central interior of British Columbia in Canada, has had to hone these traits since starting her own training business a few years ago, and it hasn't been easy. After leaving the corporate world, Kellie transitioned her career gradually by working at the Skills Centre, a training broker of sorts. "I didn't have to go out and find the work myself, but it was like having my own business in that I had to manage my office, my time, and my rates," she says.

Once she did have to find work on her own, life as a sole proprietor became a bit bumpy for Kellie, and her perseverance was tested. "When I did my initial market research, I was given phenomenally positive feedback on the need for what I provided in the business community," she says. "But the reality was, no one was willing to pay for my services. I had to go back and revisit my approach many times."

Networking was also an uphill struggle for Kellie. "I really tried to market myself through the Chamber of Commerce and my local human resources association, but those organizations didn't provide the right opportunities for me. I wish I'd known how difficult it would be to open doors. When you put the sign out that says you're 'open for business,' you're truly alone."

When I worked in interactive marketing, I had a friend, Carrie, who was the best salesperson in our entire division. She brought in many blue-chip clients single-handedly. Carrie's success led her to the decision to form her own spin-off company. After all, if she was bringing in all the business, why not keep all the revenue instead of handing over the majority to our employer? It seemed to make sense, except that Carrie underestimated how much of her motivation came from boss-imposed deadlines. When she was working from home alone, she spent way too much time watching YouTube videos. Her productivity plummeted.

So Kellie struggled with the interpersonal demands associated with being self-employed, and Carrie didn't have enough self-discipline. If you're considering entrepreneurship or sole proprietorship, you must be willing to take a hard look at yourself and see if it's a good fit—not just in theory but in practice. Let's start now.

What characteristics do you possess that would make you a strong entrepreneur or sole proprietor? What characteristics might make this lifestyle a challenge for you?

_____

_____

_____

_____

Office Politics Without the Office

Baby boomer Mike Cleary grew up in an idyllic setting in the suburbs of Richmond, Virginia. His Depression-era parents reinforced the importance of education and hard work, and Mike attended the academically rigorous Washington and Lee University. He joined the military, choosing the challenging infantry and Airborne Ranger training routes, and then settled down in a corporate job in the sales and marketing field.

Like many people I interviewed for this chapter, Mike was frustrated by office politics and thought he would be free from them if he started his own company. So he purchased one new franchise and one existing franchise from its previous owner. As he was getting his new business up and running, Mike found himself mired in problems with vendors and suppliers. "It seemed very one-sided, with many commitments and obligations on my part, and much less required of the people I was buying from," he says.

In a good faith gesture, Mike agreed to extend credit to a client who had done business with the prior owner. The client defaulted in the second month, resulting in $75,000 of lost revenue and $40,000 in lost capital. Mike also had his share of difficulties with employees. "It was a harsh wake-up call to find out how many employees are not truly committed to the business they're working for," he says. "No matter how much I tried to implement a system that would produce big incentive payouts and a working environment that would be the envy of the industry, most people just wanted a paycheck. They didn't look past their own personal wants of the moment."

When the recent recession hit, Mike saw his small business revenue disappear, and with it, his cash flow. He stretched out his payments to suppliers until he could no longer meet his obligations. His business folded. Today, Mike says that he would only own a company again if he could run the whole business by himself.

I don't think most would-be entrepreneurs recognize that office politics are everywhere, and that there is more at stake when the business is your own. Even if you're a sole proprietor, you have to cope with disrespectful, flaky, or even backstabbing clients and partners. Escaping office politics is not a good reason to ditch corporate America to start your own business. The sad truth is, unless you intend to open up shop on an alien planet, you'll never get away from classic human behavior, and as an employee-turned-entrepreneur you're simply going to trade one set of interpersonal headaches for another.

The Three Little Ps You Take for Granted

There are some things about corporate jobs that we forget about, things that we don't truly value until we don't have them anymore. These are the three little Ps—peace, prestige, and perks.

Peace is what you get when you are one player in a cast of thousands. Says Mark Herschberg: "An employee lives in a relatively safe box. He can show up to work, do his job, and go home at the end of the day having collected a paycheck. Generally the employee doesn't have to worry about where that paycheck is coming from or if it will be there tomorrow. He can focus solely on job-related tasks. If your project fails at your $2 billion company, the project gets canceled and you move on to the next one. But if it happens at your start-up, you're out of business."

Even if you work long hours employed at a large organization, you don't put in as many hours as the average entrepreneur. You are better able to leave your work agita at the office and disconnect your smartphone without the business crashing down. You are given weeks of vacation that you are encouraged to take, and you can go out to dinner with your significant other or take a mental health day that you can spend watching daytime talk shows and eating Ben & Jerry's. A more narrow set of job responsibilities means that you can focus on doing your job extremely well and let the rest of the company take care of itself.

Most corporate employees have a set career path and can reliably predict where their career will be in five or ten years. Their organizations are very explicit about how they should present themselves, how they should behave, and what rules and processes they should follow. There is something safe, comforting, and *peaceful* about clear expectations and a set structure.

Let's tackle *prestige* next. If you are a smart cookie with great interpersonal skills, with time you can get to a very good place in the corporate world. You can get a job at a top-tier company whose name you will be proud to share on your resume and on dates with a new love interest or friend. Your parents will understand what you do and be proud of you. When you spend a certain number of years at a firm with excellent name recognition, the credibility of that firm will provide more career options for life.

If your ego is important to you, a job at a large organization will be easier on it. Even if you are one of the lucky few whose small business doesn't fail in the first few years, it is likely you won't be a bona fide success either. Most entrepreneurs and sole proprietors don't accrue fame or wealth. If you want the former, go on reality TV and get your fifteen minutes. If you want the latter, work your butt off for somebody else in big business.

And finally, there are the *perks*. In today's world, the money your employer contributes to your health insurance and retirement plan is a major benefit. Have you ever tried to fund these completely on your own? I'll tell you from personal experience—it's scary. And although beefy bonuses seem to be a thing of the past, the other goodies a large organization throws into your compensation package add up. Depending on your company, you could have access to free or discounted gym memberships, child care, on-the-job lunches and dinners, retail products, cars, entertainment venues, and vacations.

Being employed at a large company also brings with it a benefit that can't be quantified, and that's access. From a networking perspective, you will have the opportunity to meet and interact with individuals with valuable knowledge and contacts that can help you drive your career forward. You may have the chance to become part of an official mentoring program, which will formalize your relationship with a more senior colleague. As a representative of a major organization, you will be introduced to representatives of other major organizations, and your professional network will take off more quickly than if you had tried to build it as an entrepreneur. Since everything that happens in the work world happens because of the people you know, this perk is priceless.

The Happiness Question Revisited

I've talked a lot about happiness in this book, so I'm sure you're wondering—who does research say is happier: entrepreneurs/sole proprietors or employees? According to Karen Klein of *Business Week*, the answer is mixed. Bill Gartner, professor of entrepreneurship at the University of Southern California's Marshall School of Business, told Klein of his conclusion. "Entrepreneurs as a group are not necessarily happier or unhappier than employees. People think that entrepreneurs have more freedom and independence than employees, but to a great extent, the company and the customers tend to control the entrepreneur, even if a boss doesn't. And the fact is, there are huge numbers of very happy employees in the world."

The Middle Ground: Intrapreneurship

I first learned about the concept of intrapreneurship from renowned business author Guy Kawasaki. An intrapreneur, defined as someone who develops a process or product within the context of a large organization, uses the resources and capabilities of the larger firm to turn a good idea into a profitable reality. In this way, he straddles the divide between a yes-man who is frustrated by his lack of power and an entrepreneur who must bear an extreme amount of risk.

Whether you're considering going out on your own eventually or you realize after reading this chapter that you don't have the stomach for it, intrapreneurship can be a great way to use your creativity and business acumen to further your career. The first step to becoming an intrapreneur is to use your knowledge of the organization to devise a concept that will address a critical need or weakness.

Next you should do your background research and outline your idea on paper if it's a process, or design a prototype if it's a product. Because company executives are often reluctant to implement new ideas in the interest of preserving the status quo, it's important to be able to demonstrate how and why your idea works, and how and why it will directly affect the organization's bottom line.

When it comes to gaining support for your idea, don't go it alone. The more colleagues you can bring on board, the better. Build an internal network by looking for individuals who share your passion for innovation and have the ear of senior managers

in the departments you'll need to work with to facilitate imple-
mentation.

Before you schedule a meeting with your boss and/or other
executives, practice positioning your idea using language they
understand—the language of profit. Speak in terms of return on
investment, cost savings, or productivity savings.

If the higher-ups buy into your idea, you may be given the
chance to launch a new product or process. However, if they don't,
all is not lost. A lot of the fun of intrapreneurship is coming up
with the next big thing, so don't give up right away. Start smaller
or go in a different direction and see how your next concept is received. You may also have more luck joining an internal committee
that has been tasked with innovation or idea generation.

If you look up intrapreneurship online, you'll read some famous examples from well-known companies such as Google and
3M. But the best individual example I've heard is from thirty-
eight-year-old Avi Deitcher of New York, who created a wireless
messaging service while he was doing information technology
work for a global financial firm.

"I was tasked with improving work flow, and I discovered that
both my internal and external customers were spending huge
amounts of money on unreliable forms of wireless messaging,"
Avi says. "Given that the number of messages being transferred
per year was in the millions, I thought senior management would
appreciate my efforts to develop a new service that would guarantee fast delivery and reduce the per-message cost by 50 to 75
percent."

Avi built the system and then piloted it with back-office

operations staff. Before he knew it, it rapidly caught on with front-office staff looking to communicate more efficiently with customers. He credits his success with a keen understanding of how his company operated and how finances were managed. "The total cost of my system was upwards of $1 million, but I knew it would be killed immediately if I couldn't get the direct operations budget under the $50,000 threshold," he says. "So I stuck to the $50,000 and charged the rest of the cost to the front-office business units."

Avi is a terrific example of someone who possesses many of the traits necessary to be an accomplished entrepreneur, but who was able to achieve so much more with the backing of a powerful organization. There are lots of Avis out there, and that's why I get frustrated when people insist on saying that the answer to career satisfaction is to abandon the corporate world. In our society, where most people are still employed in conventional work settings, it's wise not to look at everything as black and white and consider an array of options, including those that involve pursuing your passion while working for someone else. I think you will find that if you keep an open mind about what's possible in your organization, you may well be able to accomplish your professional goals by staying right where you are.

MYTHBUSTER'S SUMMARY

- If you want to start a company, the motivation fueled by being bored with your work or hating your boss won't be enough. You'll have to think hard about the marketplace need your product or service addresses and be prepared to work at a variety of tasks to bring it to fruition.

- Not everyone has the personality required for entrepreneurship or sole proprietorship. People who work for themselves are confident in their own abilities and are excellent salespeople. Their self-discipline is off the charts and they don't mind when their business intrudes on their personal life.

- You won't escape office politics by leaving corporate America. Even if you're a sole proprietor, you will have to cope with disrespectful, flaky, or even backstabbing clients and partners.

- There are some things about corporate jobs that we forget about, things that we don't truly value until we don't have them anymore. These are the three little Ps—peace, prestige, and perks.

- An intrapreneur, defined as someone who develops a process or product within the context of a large organization, straddles the divide between a yes-man who is frustrated by his lack of power and an entrepreneur who must bear an extreme amount of risk.

MYTH #10

Do What You Love, and the Money Will Follow

In the late 1980s, organizational psychologist and educator Marsha Sinetar wrote a book with a catchy title that was heard around the world—*Do What You Love, the Money Will Follow.* This saying is old enough to drink. It's also still a myth.

Mignon Fogarty is known as Grammar Girl, but she wasn't always. Born in 1967 and raised in the Seattle suburbs, Mignon was strongly encouraged by her parents to be a good student. "They always told me that my job was going to school and getting good grades, so they didn't give me a lot of chores, which means that today I'm a good writer but not a very good housekeeper or cook," she says. Mignon graduated with a BA in English from the University of Washington in Seattle and went on to get an MS in biology from Stanford University. She began her career as a science writer, becoming the editor in chief for an aging website and the editorial director for GeneticHealth.com.

As a writer who especially enjoyed interviewing scientists and trying out new technologies, Mignon delved into the world of podcasting. In order to get her show *Absolute Science* off the ground, she posted messages to podcasting forums and put up flyers near the science buildings at the local colleges. "I loved doing that show and I was passionate about it, but after nearly a year it was clear that *Absolute Science* was never going to make enough money to be worth the time required to produce it," she says.

By this time, Mignon had fallen in love with podcasting, so she looked for a different type of show that would attract more attention. The idea for a podcast about grammar appealed to her because of her substantial experience in writing and editing. The *Grammar Girl* show caught on quickly. In January 2007, CNN featured Mignon and called the show a "quick and dirty success." And then Oprah came calling. Mignon appeared on *The Oprah Winfrey Show* in March 2007 as a grammar expert, answering a viewer question about the use of possessive apostrophes. The viewer thought a previous show should have been titled "Oprah's and Gayle's Big Adventure," but Mignon confirmed that "Oprah and Gayle's Big Adventure" was a correct use of compound possession.

Mignon's widespread popularity as "Grammar Girl" led to two book deals featuring her tips in print and audio format. *Grammar Girl's Quick and Dirty Tips for Better Writing* became a *New York Times* bestseller, and today Mignon has a thriving platform as a national grammar expert. She still subscribes to *New*

Scientist and reads it every week, but she learned that her love for science did not automatically translate into a viable career. Grammar is hotter than formulas, and so she rolls with it. "I think 'do what you love and the money will follow' is a myth," she says. "There are all kinds of people who follow their passion and don't make a lot of money. Some even go bankrupt. Having passion and loving something don't guarantee that you're good at it or that it will make a successful business."

Mignon's right. Passion is not a panacea. The cliché "starving artist" came about because the dream to be an artist is one that's shared by millions, and only a lucky few are able to make a living off their art or get decent-paying jobs where they can be around art. Please remember that the small number of people who do what they love and actually have the money follow are the exception rather than the rule. In a difficult economy especially, where you're competing with hundreds of similar candidates for every desirable job, it's simply not possible to select any field and expect to make a good living, despite how much you love it or even how hard you work at it. In fact, the solution for most people is to select a career that they like well enough and that also earns them enough money to pay the bills. In this chapter I'll talk about why most dream careers aren't all they're cracked up to be, and when you'd be better served keeping your hobby on the career sidelines. Then I'll delve into some ideas for incorporating your passion into your life in a more practical way, including generating a marketable business idea, pursuing your dream job on the side (or moonlighting), taking intelligent career risks, and planning financially for a new venture. And in case you're not in a position to do any of these things, I'll close with some advice for changing your perspective and loving what you do instead of doing what you love.

The True Story about Dream Careers

Tim Ferriss was a record-setting tango dancer and champion kickboxer before extolling his productivity principles in the runaway bestseller *The 4-Hour Workweek: Escape 9–5, Live Anywhere, and Join the New Rich*. In the book Tim coins the term "lifestyle design" and focuses on helping readers find ways to be more effective so that work takes up less time. I got to know him when I interviewed him about *The 4-Hour Workweek* for my *Wall Street Journal* column in 2009 and he has since become a trusted adviser and friend.

Tim wrote an intriguing article for *WebWorkerDaily* in which he talks about the concept of the dream career. "It is popular to fantasize about dream jobs, read about them, and envy those who have escaped the daily grind to revel in career nirvana. The Web offers alluring new ways of making a living, ways that may allow you to profit from your deepest passions. But how do those who have found the Promised Land really feel?" he says. "Converting passions into 'work' is the fastest way to kill those passions. Surfing two hours on a Saturday to decompress from a hard week might be heaven, but waking up at six a.m. every morning to do it forty hours per week with difficult clients is a very different animal. Mixing business and pleasure can be a psychologically toxic cocktail."

A person who is fortunate enough to start making money at her dream career often finds that the situation isn't so dreamy after all. She begins to expect that her job will fulfill her personally and professionally at all times, and when she experiences the stress that's inevitably associated with working, she may sour on the very thing she's loved all her life. For instance, a gifted musician who manages her successful band may find herself so overwhelmed with administering bookings that she prefers to spend any leisure time she has watching TV rather than practicing her instrument. And the more pressure she feels to keep the band afloat so that it can pay her mortgage, the more she may long to escape from music and do something else entirely.

If you believe that there's only one perfect job out there for you, and that once you find it you'll jump out of bed with excitement every day, you may be in for disappointment. For one thing, no job will thrill you 100 percent of the time. As I like to say, every job has its ups and downs, aspects that we love and aspects that we don't love. There will be times when even the most wonderful job has you wishing you could hang up the Closed sign and call it a day.

Before you buy into the concept of a dream career too readily, consider this: do you really think there's just one job out there that you can do incredibly well? There are literally millions of vocations, so there must be at least a few dozen that you could do proficiently in a state of emotional contentment and financial security. Also, don't fall into the trap of assuming that there's an objective definition of a dream job, or that a terrific job situation must involve something you're passionate about, because that may not be the case. In fact, one of the happiest employees I ever met was a night janitor. He told me that cleaning office buildings was a dream job because it paid well, allowed him to work in peace and quiet, and got him home in time to see his children off to school in the morning.

When to Keep It a Hobby

One of the major problems with "do what you love, and the money will follow" is that often the things we genuinely love to do don't pay anything. These activities start off as hobbies, and perhaps they should stay that way.

Because there is no specific market demand for the products or services that arise from many hobbies, businesses associated with these hobbies tend to be unprofitable. For example, my next-door neighbor creates brilliant collages from different types of paper, but because she knows that few people would spend the money to hang a collage in the living room, she maintains a stable career as a restaurant manager.

In an article he wrote for Entre-Propel.com, Matt Thomas agrees with Tim Ferriss that hobbies don't always translate into jobs. "There is no guarantee that a hobby will translate into a set of tasks that you enjoy. Let's pretend you enjoy keeping fish as pets. Does caring for fish mean you will enjoy running a retail store? You might hate writing about fish, teaching about fish care or installing fish tank equipment for customers," he writes. "Turning a hobby into a business may ruin the fun of it. Pursuing what you love for gain may lead you to perform work-related tasks that you hate."

Thirty-six-year-old Monique Harris is a counselor by trade. She grew up in the San Francisco Bay Area at a time when you could still see the sea lions lounging on the pier at Fisherman's Wharf, and she pursued her education at the California State University, East Bay. Monique has always been passionate about photography. "My dad bought me my first camera when I was eleven, and boy, did I have fun clicking away and alternating between the limited zooming options," she says. "When I got older, though, I realized that owning my own camera wasn't so exciting when (a) I had to pay to get the film developed and (b) I did not receive a weekly allowance."

After receiving a master's degree in education, Monique took a job with Jewish Vocational Services in San Francisco to build her career counseling skills. She has spent her entire career in the education and counseling arena and is currently living in Raleigh, North Carolina, where she works for Duke University's Talent Identification Program. "Essentially, I am a counselor who prepares students for the college admissions process," she says.

And what about photography? Monique admits that she was discouraged from pursuing photography as a full-time career because of the competitiveness of the field and the expense of training. Now a working mom who travels frequently for her job, she recognizes the need for a creative outlet, but she's not willing to make all the sacrifices and life changes that would be required for a professional photography career. "This summer, I decided to purchase my first SLR camera, but I don't have the most expensive equipment. I shoot people at their homes to avoid the costs of studio lighting," she says. "I love having this hobby outside my nine-to-five. It reminds me of how important it is to have balance in my life instead of giving all my energy to work and family."

Monique may not make a boatload of money from photography, but she doesn't need to. She values the role she plays in the education sector and the financial rewards that come with it.

How to Generate a Marketable Idea

It's easier to earn money doing what you love when other people love it as much as you do. One way to ensure that's the case is to come up with a marketable business idea that you and your future customers feel passionate about.

Forty-seven-year-old John Scardapane grew up in southern New Jersey and started working in the restaurant industry in his early teens. As a chef at a local country club, John observed that the pantry station in the kitchen was always stocked with groupings of vegetables and lettuce fresh cut for the salads. He thought that if customers could see this arrangement, they might be inspired to make their own salads. At the same time, John realized that there were no healthy alternative food offerings for customers who didn't have time to sit down at the club. A former athlete and health-conscious eater himself, John imagined the concept of a restaurant that served made-to-order, entrée-sized salads.

In 1986, John pitched the Saladworks idea to a New Jersey mall, but the management was skeptical of the salad-only business model and worried that it wouldn't be profitable. "But as I sat in the food court and watched the huge numbers of people being served, I knew there was an open market just waiting to be tapped," John says. "I stuck with the idea and pursued a spot in the court, and Saladworks became the highest-grossing offering there."

From the day that he first envisioned the Saladworks concept, John has focused fanatically on his customers—why they're at the restaurant, what will satisfy them, and what will make them feel special inside and outside the Saladworks doors. "Our first priority is living up to our commitments and keeping our promises," he says. "Our customers make this business run and we have to be sure they come first at all costs." This customer-centric model has served Saladworks well. Six years after the New Jersey food court debut, John took Saladworks on the road and opened franchises all over the United States. According to *Entrepreneur* magazine, Saladworks is currently the nation's number one salad franchise and has over one hundred locations. John expects to double the number of locations in the next five years, all the while tweaking the concept to reflect changing customer attitudes and preferences.

The first rule of a marketable idea is that it will solve a pervasive customer problem. Although it's important to pursue a concept that you can dedicate your career to, it's equally essential that you think about what the market needs. You will not be able to earn a good living if there are just a handful of people who feel as strongly about your product or service as you do. Starting a new business is time-consuming and expensive, so your idea should be one that makes a lot of people care because it cures their pain right now. John Scardapane, for example, could have opened a gourmet restaurant—after all, that was his training—but he recognized that food court customers were hungry for an option that didn't force them to sacrifice their waistlines for convenience. Saladworks was successful because it bridged John's own passion for food with a strategy that appealed to millions of customers.

To learn more about the science of developing good ideas, I turned to Chip Heath, coauthor of *Made to Stick: Why Some Ideas Survive and Others Die.* Heath, who is also a business professor at Stanford University and has done a lot of research on this subject, says that sustainable ideas are credible and easy to understand. For example, if you were an engineer pitching a foreign concept like a new energy grid, you could make it more relatable by saying that it's "like an interstate highway system for energy particles."

Heath also advises us to be careful of falling into the curse of the knowledge trap. "Experts can't imagine what it's like not to have their level of knowledge, so their messages go over people's heads," he says. Instead, develop two concrete examples of what you're talking about, and then "test them out on a friend or family member who's not in your field."

What if you have trouble coming up with the big ideas? Heath has an interesting suggestion. You can make it easier by narrowing your focus, or thinking *inside* the box—it's much more manageable to brainstorm a list of white things in your fridge than it is to brainstorm in general. Another idea is to piggyback your idea on a concept that's already successful and attracts the demographic you want to target. Let's say you want to hold a fundraiser for a nonprofit you care about but aren't sure where to start.

Why not look at the organization's history to determine—and then mimic—the type of event that has attracted the greatest interest in the past?

The Trend of Moonlighting

According to the U.S. Department of Labor, one in seventeen American adults (or about 8 million people) currently work more than one job, and in the next two decades, these numbers are projected to increase. The Department of Labor reports that while moonlighters come from every demographic group, most are married, Caucasian, and in their thirties and forties. Midwestern states have the highest numbers of moonlighters, while southeastern states like Florida and Georgia have the lowest. Nearly all moonlighting has some sort of financial incentive—people either do it to meet expenses, pay off debt, or earn extra money, or they do it so they can make money while building up a business or pursuing a hobby.

Managing multiple jobs is challenging and exhausting—some moonlighters work up to eighty hours a week. But when you consider the danger inherent in dropping everything to go after your dream gig, moonlighting can be a good, low-risk compromise. Since most employers don't expect that you will devote 100 percent of your waking hours to them, holding down a job that provides a consistent paycheck and health and retirement benefits while you pursue your passion in your free time often makes sense.

Some would-be moonlighters are concerned that starting an

independent endeavor while working full-time is against the law. In the *New York Times*, Matt Villano reports that if your new business is unrelated to your current job, you are probably safe. However, if the new enterprise operates in the same industry, you may face a legal issue. "Employers can sue an employee for starting a business if the employee has taken intellectual property without permission or violated a noncompete agreement. Generally, however, unless malicious intent has been established, judges will not rule against entrepreneurial spirit," Craig Annunziata, a partner at Fisher and Phillips, comments in the *Times* article. "Judges hate to stifle people trying to better themselves."

While it may not be illegal, it is definitely unethical for moonlighters to pursue side gigs while on the clock for their day jobs. Along those lines, please make sure that you fulfill all the responsibilities that you were hired to do. If you need to complete tasks for your side gig during the business day, use your lunch hour and either leave the office or use your cell phone in a conference room. Don't take advantage of your company's trust by using company resources like its computers, its FedEx account, or the copy machine for your own venture—this could be construed as stealing and lead to trouble down the road. And if you can help it, keep your moonlighting life to yourself. Since most employment is at-will, meaning that either party can terminate the arrangement without liability, your boss could fire you if she suspects that you're losing focus on the job or are putting plans in place to change your career. Randall Hansen of QuintCareers.com, a career expert I've been following since I was researching my first book seven years ago, offers these additional tips for people thinking about moonlighting:

- **Check your main employer's policies.** Before you look for a second job, find out if your primary company has rules about holding outside employment.

- **Consider a trial basis.** Moonlighting in short doses—to accomplish some short-term goals—usually works better than working multiple jobs for long stretches.

- **Find jobs that are geographically close to each other or to your home.** Your time will be limited enough without adding a long commute to your second job.

- **Reduce your load.** If you are working multiple jobs, it's probably time to cut some of those extracurricular activities.

In order to make moonlighting work, you will need to simultaneously and slavishly manage both job schedules. Keep conflicts to a minimum by using company-provided vacation and personal days, and consider enlisting a friend, family member, or even part-time employee to cover for you at your side gig in the event that something unexpected comes up at your day job. And because moonlighting is undoubtedly a stressful lifestyle, set aside at least a few hours a week to spend with your loved ones. This will prevent your personal relationships from suffering too much and help stave off burnout.

One of the happiest moonlighters I talked to was Von Babasin, the son of Harry Babasin, one of the most famous jazz bassists of the twentieth century and an originator of the style of jazz known as bossa nova. He was also one of the only bassists of his time to lead his own group, Harry Babasin and the Jazzpickers, and he served as the producer of his own jazz label, Nocturne Records.

Von earns income by operating an apartment building in Los Angeles. It's in one of the nicest parts of L.A., Studio City, which has allowed his sons to go to the best schools the area has to offer. The job also provides Von the freedom to pursue filmmaking, a career he has enjoyed since he was in his early twenties.

As the son of a famous musician, Von received many opportunities growing up. Nevertheless, he wanted to make it on his own, so at the age of twenty-one, he took a job in craft services at Universal Studios. Shortly thereafter, an independent record label hired Von as a production manager and director for its music video division. "As a music video director, I earned an independent screening nomination for the video 'Blast' at the 1984 MTV/Billboard Music Video Conference, now known as the MTV Awards," he says. Von continued to work in film production as well, earning credits on movies such as the 1980s hit *La Bamba*.

Once his father died, however, Von was motivated to use his filmmaking talent to honor his father's career. "There are millions of fans of bossa nova around the world, hundreds of thousands of artists that play bossa nova, international festivals devoted to bossa nova, yet how many people know that Harry Babasin was the one who started the craze?" he says. "My father defined the West Coast jazz movement. How could I not feel strongly about showcasing his accomplishments?" While keeping his apartment management job, Von sent the New York Foundation for the Arts a twenty-page proposal seeking sponsorship for a Harry Babasin documentary. An agreement was signed within two weeks, and Von got to work organizing photographs, awards, recordings, and film clips with the likes of Charlie Parker, Benny Goodman, and Louis Armstrong. He's in the process of setting up interviews with the musicians from his father's era who are still living, as well as jazz historians and disc jockeys. "I realize that any documentarian could make this film, but I will tell it in a way that only I can," he says.

Von is the first to admit that his moonlighting life hasn't been easy. "I am a man of simple means. I'm not a social climber and don't need to keep up with my neighbors, but at the same time I've forced my family to accept a less extravagant lifestyle whether they like it or not," he says. "I've never owned a home or had the ability to buy one, and my job choices prevent me from sending my sons to top colleges." But in the end, Von feels that what he's doing is worth it. "My father died a month before I got married, so neither of my boys got a chance to meet him. Through this film, my sons will get to know the powerful creative impact he made on the world."

Taking Calculated Risks

Both Shari Storm and her husband, Dave, have pursued careers that they love, but not at the expense of their family's financial welfare. This is, Shari believes, an important distinction.

Forty-year-old Shari grew up in Kennewick, a midsized town

in eastern Washington. She received an undergraduate degree at the University of Washington and an MBA at Seattle University. Shari launched her career at a nonprofit credit counseling service and, for six years, traveled around the state teaching money management classes. "I never specifically wanted to work in marketing or in the financial industry, but in 1998 a colleague insisted I interview with Bill Hayes, CEO of Verity Credit Union, and he really impressed me," says Shari. She has been working there ever since.

Shari met her husband, Dave, and they had a baby girl. Dave had a job at a software training company and was bored with the work. "I'm the one who realized that Dave had to quit," she says. "He was in a position where he didn't hate it enough to leave, but didn't love it enough to thrive. The film industry, on the other hand, was something he wanted to throw himself into."

They began to plan for Dave's transition. Shari's financial career had allowed for substantial savings over the years, but she remained gainfully employed while Dave tested the waters, taking classes at a Seattle film school and trying his hand at location scouting and management jobs. "Once Dave started making money and doing interesting things like eating lunch with the stars of *Grey's Anatomy* and getting picked up from our house in a helicopter, I began to think more critically about my own career," Shari says. "I've loved writing since I was in grade school, and I thought I could make money with a book that combined my experiences as a mother and young executive." She published *Motherhood Is the New MBA: Using Your Parenting Skills to Be a Better Boss* in 2008. Shari and Dave now had three jobs between the two of them and were raising young children at the same time.

In Shari's opinion, taking an initial, calculated risk was critical. "It wasn't easy for us to stomach Dave quitting a full-time, stable job. But it wasn't practical for Dave to moonlight in location scouting, so it was all or nothing, feast or famine." Following that decision, the family moved closer to Shari's job so that they could make sure that the family's biggest income source received priority. Publishing and promoting her book while still employed at the credit union was an additional gamble, so Shari has learned to be very disciplined about the writing projects she takes on. "Many people have asked if I intend to write a second book, and my response is, 'Only if the first book makes money. I won't take the time away from my children unless it will pay for their orthodontia.'"

If Shari and Dave had simply expected the money to follow them into film and writing, they likely would have sacrificed their family's well-being and caused the unit undue stress. On the other hand, if they hadn't taken any risks at all, they would still be stuck in careers that didn't fulfill them, and as author Bill Treasurer says in *Right Risk*, that isn't a good option either. "Every risk can be split in two—the risk of action and the risk of inaction. Too often we assume that inaction is the safer path, but it can be a slow-acting gas that, at some point, can render us unconscious."

Bill Treasurer defines a "Right Risk" as the application of courage or courage in action, and a "Wrong Risk" as the application of foolishness or foolishness in action. So how do you decide if a risk is courageous or foolish? One of my early mentors, Harry Chambers, says in his book *Getting Promoted: Real Strategies for Advancing Your Career* that risks shouldn't be taken impulsively. Think about a current career risk you are considering taking, and ask yourself the following questions:

What do I want to do and why is it risky?

_____

_____

_____

_____

What is the potential upside? Will a positive outcome enhance my satisfaction with my career?

_____

_____

_____

_____

What is the potential downside? Would the worst-case scenario have a negative impact on my current or future career?

_____

_____

_____

_____

How much risk am I comfortable with? Would a lack of success be a permanent hindrance or a bump in the road?

_____
_____
_____
_____

How will I know if the risk starts to go bad? Will I be able to identify problems early enough to prevent career-damaging failure?

_____
_____
_____
_____

How will I handle a negative outcome? What is my contingency plan if the risk isn't successful?

_____
_____
_____
_____

Including others in your risk assessment will increase the chances that you will be making a responsible decision. In addition to discussing your options with family and friends who will be directly affected, consider talking to people who have taken similar career risks to see what insights and lessons they can offer.

Preparing Your Finances for a New Venture

Thirty-four-year-old Nicole Bohorad became deeply committed to helping other new parents after a traumatic experience giving birth to her daughter after just twenty-six weeks of pregnancy. But as a graduate of the University of Pennsylvania Wharton School and the New York University Stern School of Business, Nicole knew better than to abandon her well-paying sales job with NBA.com for her new website, Parentville.com. "The main reason it wasn't practical to make money off my passion right away was because the economy was poor and jobs in the digital and parenting spaces were being taken by people who were experts in the field," she relates. She continued working full-time at NBA.com in order to pay her family's bills and invest in her new business gradually.

Instead of doing what you love and assuming the money will follow, think about your career transition objectively. Planning is everything, so go online and talk to people in your prospective industry to determine how long it will take you to get up and running in your new career, and how much you will need to spend on additional schooling, training, and other professional development activities. Assess how much you can expect to earn in your first few years in the field, and don't forget to take into account health care expenses. If your current employer provides medical benefits, calculate the costs of continuing that coverage with COBRA.

Now is also the time to start paying close attention to your spending. Create a spreadsheet in your smartphone that allows you to keep track of where your money is going on a daily basis. If you do this for a month or even just for a few weeks, you'll be amazed at the data you'll accumulate. You'll start to see patterns of unnecessary spending (your morning Starbucks run, sushi takeout, etc.) and areas where you can tighten your belt. A great question to ask is: "Do I really need this?" If you honestly don't, then put the money away for your career change.

It's generally a good idea to create a reserve of cash that can float you for six months as you actively pursue your new career. Susan Tompor of the *Detroit Free Press* offers these smart ideas for finding the money for such a fund:

- Reconsider monthly services like your cell phone and gym membership—cancel what you don't need and renegotiate what you do.

- Get into the habit of putting 5 to 10 percent of each paycheck into savings.

- Buy U.S. savings bonds (a Series I savings bond earns 3.36 percent for the first six months).

- If you want season tickets for a sports team or local theater, set up a system to split the costs/tickets with someone else.

- Take advantage of restaurant and store loyalty programs and plan purchases to use rebates, discounts, and Groupons (www.groupon.com).

If your fund still comes up short, you might pick up some extra income via a holiday retail gig, freelance work, or an eBay sale. Getting out of debt will be helpful too. Especially when it comes to credit cards, people have the tendency to bury their heads in

the sand while their debts get bigger and bigger. If you're thinking about making a career change and you don't want to go broke
doing it, then you have to nip this one in the bud. The first step is
to call each financial institution you have debt with and try to
negotiate a lower interest rate of 5 to 12 percent. I recommend trying to get transferred to the retention department, because they
are the ones concerned with keeping you as a customer and not
losing you to the competition.

As for paying off the balances you have, make the minimum
required payments every month—by the deadline—and spend as
much remaining money as possible paying off one account at a
time. Don't open any new credit cards or use your existing cards
for cash advances or to buy big-ticket items you can't afford in their
entirety. For in-depth guidance, I suggest asking close friends and
family members to recommend a financial planner. In addition to
helping you get out of debt, a certified planner can assist you with
managing your money in the most effective way and making the
right type of investments in your new career.

I am often asked about the best way to secure outside funding
for a new business idea. There are entire books devoted to this
subject, but all I'll say here is that you have to be prepared to do
lots of thinking about your idea before you start asking people for
money to fund it (even if they're family members who have the
utmost faith in you). Substantial market research, a comprehen-
sive business plan, and projected costs and income are all neces-
sities, and most new entrepreneurs retain the services of a small
business attorney from the very beginning. For information on
the type of loans you can apply for and the organizations you can
approach, check out the following resources:

- Business Know-How (www.businessknowhow.com)

- Business Owner's Toolkit (www.toolkit.com)

- *Entrepreneur* magazine (www.entrepreneur.com)

- StartupNation (www.startupnation.com)

- U.S. Small Business Administration (www.sba.gov)

Love What You Do (Instead of the Other Way Around)

As I talked about at the beginning of the chapter, it is very likely that you could be happy doing a wide variety of jobs. In an article he wrote for Kiplinger.com, career expert Marty Nemko suggests that the best path for most people is to pick a nonglamorous career with these characteristics:

- Moderate challenge

- Meaningful work

- A kind, competent boss

- Pleasant co-workers

- Learning opportunities

- Reasonable pay

- Reasonable work hours

- A short commute

Nemko says that a job with even half of these will make you more likely to love your job than if you had pursued a long-shot career. He also tells us that finding career contentment is often a matter of diving in wholeheartedly to whatever job is available. Nemko shares the story of Gary, a young man who recently graduated from Michigan State with no clue what he wanted to do. His cousin told him that a job was open in a dashboard manufacturing plant. Gary wasn't passionate about dashboards; who is? But he was tired of living on his parents' sofa, so he took the job. Because he was bright and curious, he asked lots of questions and soon became the go-to guy on the factory floor. Soon after that, Gary got a promotion and a raise and felt genuinely excited about his future in the industry.

Apparently, feeling expert at something—even something as mundane as dashboards—and being recognized for that expertise, is more likely to create career passion than going after a lottery-odds career. So instead of doing what you love and expecting the money to follow, why not pick or stay with a job that already pays well and find ways to create a more meaningful work experience?

Throughout this book, I've addressed several ways to fully realize the potential and promise of the job you currently have, such as becoming a recognized spokesperson on a topic of expertise, developing a new product or service with your company's support, and adjusting your at-work thinking patterns and banishing irrational expectations. Here are some additional suggestions to take to heart as you strive to "love what you do":

- **Reengage emotionally.** Imagine you are one of the hundreds of people who apply for jobs with your organization every day. What is going through these candidates' minds? What do they view about your job as desirable? Think back to when you first started your job. Pretend it's your first day and echo your initial enthusiasm for your work.

- **Look outside your box.** Forget for a minute that you had to be dragged to your company's last training seminar. Think about the skills you want to develop in your career over the long term, and sniff around your organization to see how you might get them launched and paid for in the form of classroom instruction, job rotation, lateral moves, sabbaticals, or volunteering.

- **Become a mentor.** Research has shown that we enjoy our work more when we have an opportunity to teach it to others. Contact your HR department and sign up for your organization's formal mentorship program if there is one. If not, volunteer to mentor a younger colleague and you may learn a thing or two from her about finding meaning on a less-than-perfect career path.

MYTHBUSTER'S SUMMARY

- The cliché "starving artist" came about because the dream to be an artist is one that's shared by millions, and only a lucky few are able to get decent-paying work doing it. It's simply not possible to select any field and expect to make a good living, regardless of how much you love it or even how hard you work at it.

- Because there is no specific market demand for the products or services that arise from many hobbies, businesses associated with these hobbies tend to be unprofitable.

- It's easier to earn money doing what you love when other people love it as much as you do. And one way to ensure that's the case is to come up with a marketable business idea that you and your future customers feel passionate about.

- When you consider the danger inherent in simply dropping everything to go after your dream gig, moonlighting—or pursuing your passion during your time off from a more lucrative day job—can be a good, low-risk compromise.

- Finding career contentment is often a matter of diving in wholeheartedly to whatever job is available. The mind is a powerful tool, and changing the way you think about your job's potential could very well alter the reality of your situation.

AFTERWORD

If, before starting this book, you bought into one or more of these myths, I don't want you to be too hard on yourself. At some point I too believed in at least half of them, and when my supervisors tried to educate me, I didn't listen, because I too was plagued by blind spots. But over time, the warped point of view that resulted from my false beliefs caused me a great deal of unhappiness. For example, when I felt that everyone else was getting promoted faster than I was, I was jealous, and when I was convinced that corporate America was killing me a little bit each day, I was bitter and frustrated.

Many of these myths took root in the old business world, when there was a much greater emphasis on climbing over the people in front of you to meet your destiny. And if there's one message I hope you've received from this book, it's that all that has changed. While office politics will always exist, today you don't have to worry as much about the colleague trying to steal your promotion or how to manipulate your boss into thinking you're performing better than you are. You just have to be a good human being.

Truly understanding how business works took me years of difficult experiences and hardships, but I feel fortunate that I'm able to call out all of these myths in my early thirties. Many people I interviewed for this book were much older and in the twilight of their careers before they learned the lessons they needed to be successful. I hope you are as inspired by them as I was.

Like the rest of my books, *Blind Spots* is grounded in best practices. As an imperfect individual, you will not be able to adhere to 100 percent of this guidance 100 percent of the time. However, I hope that you will remember these myths and their realities when you are faced with challenging situations in your working life, and that you will pass on anything you construe as wisdom to your younger or more inexperienced colleagues, friends, and family members.

Rather than being discouraged by these myths, I hope learning the truth about them has empowered and energized you to take the next step in your career and develop the traits, skills, and attitudes that will be critical of a business leader in the twenty-first century. I wish you all the success and satisfaction in the world.

BIBLIOGRAPHY

Chapter 1

Buchheit, Paul. "Overnight Success Takes a Long Time." 2009. http://paulbuchheit
.blogspot.com/2009/01/overnight-success-takes-long-time.html.

Chabris, Christopher, and Daniel Simons. *The Invisible Gorilla: And Other Ways Our
Intuitions Deceive Us*. New York: Crown, 2010.

Gladwell, Malcolm. *Outliers: The Story of Success*. New York: Little, Brown, 2008.

Johnson, Vic. "Goal Setting: Pops Proves It's Never Too Late." GetMotivation.com,
2005. http://www.getmotivation.com/goals/vjohnson-pops-goal.html.

Kai, Jai. "How to Set the Highest Goals and Be Successful." 2009. http://www
.content4reprint.com/personal-development/goal-setting/how-to-set-the
-highest-goals-and-be-successful.htm.

Tierney, John. "For Good Self-Control, Try Getting Religious About It." *New York
Times*, 2008. http://www.nytimes.com/2008/12/30/science/30tier.html?fta=y.

Wax, Dustin. "The Science of Setting Goals." Lifehack.org, 2008. http://www.life
hack.org/articles/productivity/the-science-of-setting-goals.html.

Chapter 2

The 2009 Edelman Trust Barometer. Edelman.com. http://www.edelman.com/
trust/2009/.

American Psychological Association. "What Makes a Good Leader: The Assertiveness Quotient." Apa.org, 2007. http://www.apa.org/news/press/releases/2007/02/
good-leaders.aspx.

Covey, Stephen M. R. *The Speed of Trust: The One Thing That Changes Everything*. New
York: Free Press, 2008.

Foster, Stuart. "The Downside of Being Provocative." The Lost Jacket blog, 2009.
http://thelostjacket.com/marketing/downside-provocative.

Joel, Mitch. "The Slippery Slope of Being Provocative." Six Pixels of Separation blog,
2009. http://www.twistimage.com/blog/archives/the-slippery-slope-of-being
-provocative/.

Bibliography

"Jon & Kate Plus 8." Wikipedia (retrieved August 2010). http://en.wikipedia.org/wiki/Jon_%26_Kate_Plus_8v.

Scott, Elizabeth. "Reduce Stress with Increased Assertiveness." About.com, 2006. http://stress.about.com/od/relationships/p/profileassertiv.htm.

Sonnenfeld, Jeffrey, and Andrew Ward. *Firing Back: How Great Leaders Rebound after Career Disasters*. Boston: Harvard Business School Press, 2007.

Thomas-Kilmann Conflict Mode Instrument. Mountain View, CA: CPP, 1974–2009.

Chapter 3

Balderrama, Anthony. "13 Things to Keep to Yourself at Work." CareerBuilder.com, 2009. http://www.cnn.com/2009/LIVING/worklife/02/16/cb.tmi.at.the.office/index.html.

Chensvold, Christian. "Five Rules of Style for the Business-Casual Workplace." BNET.com, 2008. http://www.bnet.com/article/five-rules-of-style-for-the-business-casual-workplace/212795.

Covey, Stephen R. *The 7 Habits of Highly Effective People*. New York: Free Press, 2004.

Przecha, Donna. "They Changed Our Name at Ellis Island." Geneology.com, 2010. http://www.genealogy.com/88_donna.html.

Tussing, Melissa. "When Your Future Doctor Has a Facebook Page." Medill News Service, 2009. http://news.medill.northwestern.edu/chicago/news.aspx?id=142783.

Chapter 4

Bates College. "April 1968: Benjamin Mays Delivers King Eulogy." Bates.edu (retrieved 2010). http://www.bates.edu/x49908.xml.

"Benjamin Mays." Wikipedia (retrieved August 2010). http://en.wikipedia.org/wiki/Benjamin_Mays.

Caruso, Denise. "Knowledge Is Power Only if You Know How to Use It." *New York Times*, 2007. http://www.nytimes.com/2007/03/11/business/yourmoney/11frame.html.

Judge, Timothy, and B. A. Scott. "The Popularity Contest at Work: Who Wins, Why, and What Do They Receive?" *Journal of Applied Psychology*, 2009. http://www.ncbi.nlm.nih.gov/pubmed/19186893.

Kristanda, Denis. "Knowledge Is Power? Sorry, Not True!" Investingbyme.com, 2010. http://investingbyme.com/9/knowledge-is-power-sorry-not-true/.

Rains, Julie. "Awesome Accomplishments: 50+ Questions to Ask Yourself and Figure Out What You've Done." WiseBread.com, 2009. http://www.wisebread.com/awesome-accomplishments-50-questions-to-ask-yourself-and-figure-out-what-youve-done.

White, Doug. "Attention, Attention: Tips for Boosting Your Visibility at Work." Monster+HotJobs, 2010. http://hotjobs.yahoo.com/career-articles-attention_attention_tips_for_boosting_your_visibility_at_work-885.

Chapter 5

Brooks, David. "The Sandra Bullock Trade." *New York Times*, 2010. http://www.nytimes.com/2010/03/30/opinion/30brooks.html.

Clark, Josh. "How the Peter Principle Works." HowStuffWorks.com, 2010. http://money.howstuffworks.com/peter-principle.htm.

Portocarrero, Carlos. "Turning Down a Promotion: A Baseball Lesson." The Writer's Coin blog, 2009. http://www.thewriterscoin.com/2009/04/30/turning-down-a-promotion/.

Gilbert, Daniel Todd. *Stumbling on Happiness*. New York: Vintage Books, 2007.

Lublin, Nancy. "Do Something: Let's Hear It for the Little Guys." *Fast Company*, 2010. http://www.fastcompany.com/magazine/144/do-something-lets-hear-it-forthe-little-guys.html.

"Michael D. Brown." Wikipedia (retrieved August 2010). http://en.wikipedia.org/wiki/Michael_D._Brown.

Chapter 6

Green, Sarah. "Investigating the Pay Gap." HBR.org, 2010. http://hbr.org/web/extras/pay-gap/1-slide.

Johnson, Gerald O., and Ellison Clary. "In Defense of Gloria Pace King." *Charlotte Post*, 2009. http://www.thecharlottepost.com/index.php?src=news&refno=1428.

WSOCTV.com. "Statement of the Board of Directors, United Way of Central Carolinas, Inc." 2008. http://www.wsoctv.com/news/17301088/detail.html.

Chapter 7

Bolt, Jim. "Coaching: The Fad That Won't Go Away." *Fast Company*, 2006. http://www.fastcompany.com/resources/learning/bolt/041006.html.

"Daniel Goleman." Wikipedia (retrieved August 2010). http://en.wikipedia.org/wiki/Daniel_Goleman.

Goleman, Daniel. "Biography." DanielGoleman.info, 2010. http://www.danielgoleman.info/biography.

"Manny Ramirez." Wikipedia (retrieved December 2010). http://en.wikipedia.org/wiki/Manny Ramirez.

Musselwhite, Chris. "Self-Awareness and the Effective Leader." Inc.com, 2007. http://www.inc.com/resources/leadership/articles/20071001/musselwhite.html.

Neill, James. "What Is Locus of Control?" Wilderdom.com, 2006. http://wilderdom.com/psychology/loc/LocusOfControlWhatIs.html.

Steinbach, Matt. "Manny Ramirez Needs to Stop Being Manny." *Foghorn* Online, 2009. http://foghorn.usfca.edu/2009/03/manny-ramirez-needs-to-stop-being-manny/.

Suster, Mark. "Never Hire Job Hoppers. Never. They Make Terrible Employees." Both Sides of the Table blog, 2010. http://www.bothsidesofthetable.com/2010/04/22/never-hire-job-hoppers-never-they-make-terrible-employees/.

Chapter 8

Clifford, Stephanie. "Condé Nast to Close *Gourmet, Cookie,* and *Modern Bride*." Media Decoder blog, 2009. http://mediadecoder.blogs.nytimes.com/2009/10/05/conde-nast-to-close-gourmet-magazine/.

————. "Condé Nast's Executive on Why the Company Closed Four Magazines." Media Decoder blog, 2009. http://mediadecoder.blogs.nytimes.com/2009/10/05/conde-nasts-townsend-on-why-the-company-closed-four-magazines/.

Conlin, Michelle. "When the Laid-Off Are Better Off." *Business Week,* 2009. http://www.businessweek.com/magazine/content/09_44/b4153065919516.htm.

"Don Imus." Wikipedia (retrieved August 2010). http://en.wikipedia.org/wiki/Don_Imus.

Greenberg, Edward S., et al. *Turbulence: Boeing and the State of American Workers and Managers.* New Haven, CT: Yale University Press, 2010.

"Ruth Reichl." Wikipedia (retrieved August 2010). http://en.wikipedia.org/wiki/Ruth_Reichl.

Chapter 9

FindLaw.com. "A Majority of Americans Have Started or Considered Starting Their Own Business, Says New FindLaw.com Survey." 2009. http://company.findlaw.com/pr/2009/032009.business.html.

Klein, Karen. "Are Entrepreneurs Happier Than Wage Slaves?" *Business Week,* 1999. http://www.businessweek.com/smallbiz/news/coladvice/ask/ak990223.htm.

Chapter 10

Business Wire. "Saladworks Named #1 Salad Franchise by *Entrepreneur* Magazine." 2010. http://www.allbusiness.com/company-activities-management/company-structures-ownership/13729287-1.html.

Chambers, Harry. *Getting Promoted: Real Strategies for Advancing Your Career.* New York: Basic Books, 1999.

Ferriss, Timothy. "The Dangerous Myth of the Dream Job." *WebWorkerDaily,* 2007. http://webworkerdaily.com/2007/05/09/the-dangerous-myth-of-the-dream-job/.

Hansen, Randall. "Moonlighting in America: Strategies for Managing Working Multiple Jobs." QuintCareers.com, 2010. http://wtww.quintcareers.com/moonlighting_jobs.html.

Nemko, Marty. "Do What You Love and Starve." Kiplinger.com, 2007. http://www.kiplinger.com/columns/onthejob/archive/2007/job1205.html.

Thomas, Matt. "Why the Saying: 'Pursue What You Love and Money Will Follow' Is Wrong." Entre-Propel.com, 2009. http://www.entre-propel.com/financial-freedom/why-the-saying-pursue-what-you-love-and-money-will-follow-is-wrong/.

Tompor, Susan. "Put Away Debt: Put Money into Savings." *Detroit Free Press,* 2010. http://www.freep.com/article/20100107/COL07/1070460/Put-away-debt—put-money-into-savings.

Treasurer, Bill. *Right Risk: 10 Powerful Principles for Taking Giant Leaps with Your Life.* San Francisco: Berrett-Koehler, 2003.

Villano, Matt. "How to Moonlight as an Entrepreneur." *New York Times,* 2006. http://www.nytimes.com/2006/10/29/jobs/29advi.html.

INDEX

Page numbers in **bold** indicate tables.

Index

Index

Index

Index

Index

Index